Operational Leadership

Operational Leadership

Andrew Spanyi

business**expert**
Press

Operational Leadership

Copyright © Andrew Spanyi, 2010.

First published in 2010 by
Business Expert Press, LLC
222 East 46th Street, New York, NY 10017
www.businessexpertpress.com

ISBN-13: 978-1-60649-112-6 (paperback)
ISBN-10: 1-60649-112-1 (paperback)

ISBN-13: 978-1-60649-113-3 (e-book)
ISBN-10: 1-60649-113-x (e-book)

10.4128/9781606491133

A publication in the Business Expert Press Strategic Management collection

Collection ISSN: 2150-9611 (print)
Collection ISSN: 2150-9646 (electronic)

Cover design by Jonathan Pennell
Interior design by Scribe, Inc.

First edition: July 2010

10 9 8 7 6 5 4 3 2 1

Printed in the United States of America.

Abstract

Operational Leadership examines the comprehensive combination of leadership and management behaviors needed to fundamentally improve how businesses get products and/or services developed, sold, delivered, and serviced. It is written for executives and graduate students and includes examples of both success and failure in improving operations, in the belief that while people are motivated by success stories, they often learn as much, or more, from the mistakes that others have made. This book integrates and extends key concepts in the literature on leadership and process management and applies them to the improvement of operational performance. The importance of viewing operations in the context of a company's key capabilities, or end-to-end processes, is emphasized where collaboration across traditional organizational boundaries is essential. It is proposed that performance-oriented organizations will come to recognize the need to appoint key senior executives as change agents, aligned with the company's core capabilities, to continuously improve and manage operational performance.

Keywords

leadership, operations, information technology, strategy, capabilities, collaboration

Contents

Preface

I first began paying attention to the role of leaders in improving operations in the mid-1980s. At the time, I was a manager at Xerox Learning Systems in Canada, and Xerox's "Leadership Through Quality" program was being rolled out. I observed then that most of the issues were just as much around leadership as around quality. Since the early 1990s, I have worked on over 140 large process-improvement projects—and again, one of the most important impediments to performance improvement has been committed leadership.

The world has changed enormously over the past 20 years. The rapid development of information technology (IT) and the impact of the World Wide Web have fundamentally changed how businesses operate. Various methods of improving operations—such as Six Sigma, Lean, Reengineering—and technology-enabled business process management (BPM) have evolved and have been applied by companies in their search for ways to improve operations in a significant and sustainable way. The body of literature on these methods, along with the literature on leading change, change management, knowledge management, and analytics, continues to evolve. The tools at the disposal of firms such as BPM, service-oriented architecture (SOA), and the "cloud" have also evolved. But the results in dramatically improving operations continue to disappoint. Fewer than 40% of major improvement projects typically achieve their stated goals, and the sustainability of these gains is even more questionable. Leadership engagement and commitment remain one of the primary culprits.

Companies have become increasingly adept at improving how work gets done within organizational boundaries. However, they still struggle when it comes to improving the broadly cross-functional activities involved in how their businesses get products and services developed, sold, delivered, and serviced. Part of the problem is the proliferation and fragmentation of improvement methods, tools, and approaches. In my view, the broad range of improvement options leads to unnecessary complexity, as companies attempt to simultaneously deploy several improvement methods without an umbrella approach.

Some executives do see the big picture. Similarly, some of the middle managers who have participated in MBA courses I've taught have become excited by the concept of organizational capabilities and practices of operational leadership. In writing this book, my intent is to elevate the key concepts of operational improvement and its related leadership practices above the hype of the various methods in vogue. This book will appeal to those who are passionate about the fundamental improvement of how their businesses get products and services developed, sold, delivered, and serviced.

I wrote this book expressly for two audiences. First, it is targeted at those executives who are frustrated with the current fragmentation of various improvement methods and are looking for a better way. It is also meant to assist those university professors who teach courses on operations to the executives of the future—students currently in MBA programs. I hope you will find this book to be useful as supplemental reading material in outlining a different, and more integrated, approach to leading operational performance improvement.

This book integrates and extends key concepts in the areas of leadership and process management. In so doing it draws upon Dr. John Kotter's seminal work in leading change and the work of the late Dr. Geary Rummler and Alan Brache on process management. Their influence on my thinking is evident in this book.

I hope you will find some of the concepts and examples thought-provoking and I welcome your comments and questions.

Andrew Spanyi
www.spanyi.com

CHAPTER 1

Introduction

Effective leadership has long been recognized as one of the elusive critical factors in organizational success, especially when it comes to improving operational performance. Customers are increasingly demanding higher levels of speed and quality, yet leaders often focus mainly on reducing the costs of operations. Yes, organizations do pay lip service to the slogan "the customer is king," but it certainly doesn't always feel that way from a customer's perspective. The data on customer satisfaction continues to disappoint. Customers were only marginally more satisfied in 2007 than in 1994, according to the American Customer Satisfaction Index, which hovered around 75% in 2007, barely above the 1994 benchmark of 74.75%. While this index did improve in 2008, the scope of improvement was marginal. If similar aggregate data on customer satisfaction was available for the business-to-business (B2B) sector, it's not likely to paint a much better picture. Nor are customer expectations likely to subside any time soon. The impact of the World Wide Web is one of the major culprits. We now demand instant information, anytime and practically anywhere. Maybe we're not quite there yet, but it probably won't be long before customers can get practically any information they want, in any form they need, at any time and place, and at zero or minimal cost.[1] In order to meet current and anticipated future challenges, what is needed is a new operational leadership mindset and paradigm that enables both breakthrough change and the discipline of continuous improvement in operations.

There's no shortage of advice on improving operational performance. Academics and researchers have advised leaders to view the business end-to-end from the customer's perspective. "Staple yourself to an order"[2] and become "easy to do business with"[3] are just two of the many recipes for success in improving operations. Consultants have provided a number of well-documented improvement methods as they urge organizations to become "lean," strive for nearly zero defects with "Six Sigma," or radically reengineer business processes through the application of information technology.

In spite of the abundance of advice and the plethora of improvement methods, the actual success rate in driving and sustaining change is dismal. Research on leading change in 1996 reported that only about 30% of change programs succeed.[4] In the 1990s, the critics of reengineering emphasized that only about a third of reengineering efforts succeed. More recently, in 2008, a broad-based survey of 3,199 executives around the world found that only one transformation in three succeeds.[5] The Standish Group's 2009 report on information technology (IT) project success indicated that only 32% of the surveyed projects were delivered on time, on budget, and with the required features and functions. A recent article also suggested that nearly 60% of all corporate Six Sigma initiatives failed to yield desired results.[6] Other studies over the past decade reveal very similar outcomes. It appears that in spite of the abundant body of knowledge on leadership and change management, companies have not had widespread success in implementing change programs.

Leadership, in general, remains problematic for most major change programs such as downsizing, rightsizing, restructuring, turnarounds, and perhaps most so with respect to transforming operations. Change programs such as downsizing, rightsizing, and restructuring are complex and do require focused leadership, if only on the short term. Operational transformation differs from many of these other major change programs insomuch as it requires not only a focused effort short term change but also an ongoing program of continuous improvement. It calls for *operational leadership*, which is the multifaceted combination of leadership and management behaviors and attitudes needed to fundamentally improve how businesses get products and services developed, sold, delivered, and serviced.

What you will gain from this book is a new way of thinking about operational leadership. It will challenge you to think differently in several ways. First, this book argues in favor of an umbrella approach to improving operational performance, which encompasses key tools from various improvement methods such as Lean, Six Sigma, Reengineering, and Process Management, yet without the quasi-religious zeal associated with several of these individual methods. Next, the book presents a set of thought-provoking principles, practices, and pitfalls of operational leadership. Finally, examples of both success and failure are presented, on the premise that people are motivated by success stories but actually learn more from mistakes that others make.

What's the Problem?

Lack of committed leadership typically surfaces among the top few barriers in practically every survey on the obstacles in successfully transforming operational performance. Why do leaders continue to struggle in this regard? There are at least three possible reasons: leaders don't care, leaders can't focus, and leaders don't know how.

The view that senior executives don't really care about operations is based on the proposition that the general business culture holds operations in low priority. Executives tend to focus on making acquisitions, planning mergers, and selling divisions. Isn't that what gets a Chief Executive Officer's (CEO) or Chief Financial Officer's (CFO) picture in the paper? Operations simply aren't sufficiently glamorous.[7] What's more, once the executive team gets busy working on strategic planning, budgeting, capital allocation, and other major issues, it's all too easy for operations to be out of sight. Traditional attitudes compound the problem with deeply held, albeit mistaken, beliefs such as "we're smarter than our customers and we know what they really need" and "our over-riding responsibility is to produce near term shareholder returns."[8] Frequent reorganizations tend to exacerbate this situation, as middle managers realign their focus from taking care of day-to-day operations to relationship building with new bosses and new peers.

Then there's the argument that executives are aware of the importance of improving operational performance and providing customers with value, but there's just too much going on to maintain the needed focus. Not only is corporate attention a zero-sum game, but executives also have a severe case of attention deficit disorder.[9] Many organizations have dozens of initiatives competing for executive attention such that project portfolio management has become a management science. Focusing on operational performance is simply yet another initiative added to the list. There's more than a grain of truth to this.

Yet another view is that leaders simply don't know how to do it. They view the business in functional or departmental terms and have a traditional bias. There are so many popular improvement methods—such as TQM, Lean, Six Sigma, Reengineering, Enterprise Resource Planning (ERP), and Customer Relationship Management (CRM)—that each takes on the flavor of the year. The growing complexity of business in general, due to factors such as globalization, regulation, and the pace of change of technology, adds yet another element into the mix such that leaders may not know how to transform operational performance in a sustainable way.

Even though business is arguably the most demanding of team sports, leadership teams typically don't practice. That is, they don't practice or role-play, as a senior management team, on how the organization performs for customers. They don't fully understand how the flow of value-added activity creates value for customers. If they knew how, wouldn't they measure what's important to customers in a disciplined way? Wouldn't they assign accountability for the performance of key capabilities in the company's value chain instead of opting to assign accountability purely in terms of functional or business unit lines? Would they not want to deploy enabling technology with a view on the degree of its positive impact on operational performance? Wouldn't they plan and implement recognition and reward systems to acknowledge the teams of people who do the most to improve operational performance? If they knew how, then they would probably attempt to do much of this.

In a nutshell, a big part of the problem is that executives continue to view the performance of the organization mainly in a departmental context. They have an ad hoc approach toward improving operations. When they launch improvements in operational performance, these initiatives are often of small scope and defined within departmental boundaries. These improvement projects may yield some benefits, but they surely leave money on the table. Traditional thinkers rarely measure what matters to customers. They go from one initiative to the next with insufficient focus on sustaining gains. They do not sufficiently appreciate that wholesale changes in organization structure and shifting priorities can disrupt the sustainment of major change.

What's Needed?

There's no magic involved in operational improvement and even in transformation. But this type of change does require a leadership and management mindset and behavior that are different from the norm. It requires that executives be fully prepared to provide customers with what they have come to expect and will increasingly demand. It also involves a fundamental shift in conventional wisdom, working collaboratively in a new way, and a higher level of competence in operational leadership. What is operational leadership? Operational leadership is defined as *the comprehensive set of leadership and management behaviors needed to fundamentally improve and manage how their businesses get products and services developed, sold, delivered, and serviced.* It relies on the following fundamental beliefs:

- The performance of shareholders is best served when an organization performs to fully satisfy the needs of its customers. This requires that leaders view the business from the "outside-in," that is, from the customer's perspective.[10]
- A company can only outperform its competitors if it can establish a difference that can be preserved by delivering greater value to customers, by creating comparable value at a lower cost, or by doing both.[11]
- An end-to-end view of operational performance invariably requires an approach that marries radical innovation and the discipline of continuous, incremental improvement. "Piecemeal approaches that are assumed to be *the* answer are as dangerous as no response at all."[12]

Basic service delivery isn't enough to differentiate an organization in today's market environment. Propelling a company beyond simple customer satisfaction to the type of relationships that can drive business growth demands a more profound understanding of the services that customers value, as well as employees who are empowered and motivated to interact with those customers the way the customers would like. That calls for viewing the business from the customer's point of view—or from the "outside-in." Drucker, considered to be the intellectual father of viewing the business from the customer's perspective, wrote of the "thick and distorting glasses" of managers, driven by too great an emphasis on an internal perspective.[13] Other authors (Tichy and Charan, Bund, and Spanyi, among others) and respected business leaders (Welch and Gerstner) have reinforced this perspective.[14] Yet the majority of today's corporations fall prey to a largely internal focus, leading to, among other things, the continued predominance of functional silos and fiefdoms.

The principal skills most frequently lacking in managers are the means for developing a view of the business in terms of the cross-functional activities that constitute the company's value chain and the means for creating value for customers. Such a viewpoint is an essential ingredient in shifting the leadership perspective from a traditional functional paradigm to more of a customer-centric perspective. This is what a firm's leaders need in order to develop a shared understanding of the company's performance in terms of its value chain, or if you will, its capabilities and business processes. Yet, to this day, when an executive is asked to draw a picture of his or her business, they sketch what looks like a traditional organization chart, with boxes and labels depicting vertical reporting relationships. But this type of schematic fails to show how the business serves its customers, the products and services offered, and the value-creating flow of work. The organization chart, by itself, cannot be measured. Accordingly, if the traditional vertical organization view is the *only view* that exists, then that impedes an organization's ability to plan, execute, and sustain significant improvement to operations.[15]

The traditional vertical view of business is the primary obstacle to success in improving operational performance. It leads to frequent reorganizations, an unprecedented level of complexity, the suboptimal deployment of IT, and contributes to poor decision making. The traditional view of business leads to an obsession with organization structure and results in frequent reorganizations, which tend to divert attention from the key operational activities that add value to the business and create value for customers. It contributes to a continuing concern around the age-old business-IT divide, due in part to an abdication of responsibility by operational business leaders for defining and actively participating in the implementation of essential, enabling information technology, on the grounds that it is the job of the IT department. Accordingly, the business value of IT systems is seldom fully realized, as the leaders of other functional areas do not develop a shared view on how much to spend on IT, where to spend the funds, and whom to blame if it doesn't work out.[16] Yet, significant improvements in operational performance increasingly rely on enabling IT.

The traditional vertical view of business also complicates decision making. As executives are primarily concerned with the performance of their departments, insufficient attention is devoted to the set of metrics that define operational performance from both the customer's and the company's perspective. The needed data sets are seldom collected, and, in the absence of operational analytics, executives resort to making key business decisions based primarily on their "gut feel," instinct, and prior experience.[17]

There are several influential reasons for the prevailing traditional view of business. First, at the time that most of today's leaders attended business school, the curriculum still reinforced a traditional, functional view of business. Next, most firms are still organized along traditional functional lines. Then, most firms still develop plans, budgets, and even recognition and reward systems along departmental lines. However, planning, executing, and sustaining significant improvement in operations requires that leaders view the business from the perspective of the customer, in terms of the performance of end-to-end workflows and in the context of a company's value chain. This view of the business can be learned and is based on a set of key skills and attitudes relating to three key areas: crafting a compelling case for change, taking action, and sustaining gains.

On the other hand, a number of factors stand in the way of learning the needed skills, not the least of which are several misleading either-or propositions, popularized in recent management literature. What's more important—strategy or execution? What is more effective—radical or incremental change? What's more essential—leadership or management? While these either-or propositions may stimulate some intellectual discussion for the management teams of large, global conglomerates at a headquarters level, the answer at the operational level is clearly that both are necessary and neither is sufficient. It's not OR—it's AND. An understanding of strategy is essential in order to plan needed improvement in operations, *and* execution is essential to success. Radical change is often needed to execute significant operational improvement, *and* incremental continuous improvement is needed to optimize and sustain changes. Leadership is indispensable in launching and taking action to improve operational performance, *and* management is essential in sustaining operational improvements.

Planning, executing, and sustaining significant improvements in operational performance do indeed require a new brand of leadership—operational leadership—in order to craft a compelling case for change, to lead in taking action, and to lead in sustaining gains. The essence of operational leadership is when a leader has willing follows who are inspired to wholeheartedly commit to a common course of action.[18] That's what this book explores.

Mapping the Chapters of This Book

Chapter 1 has introduced you to some of the key issues and challenges in improving operations and the role of leadership. It began to make the case for the importance of operational leadership, outlined some of the challenges in leading operational improvements, and proposed a set of beliefs that are fundamental to success in this respect.

Chapter 2 provides you with an overview of the principles, practices, and pitfalls of operational leadership. Here, some of the essential literature on leading change is identified. Then, selected core principles are examined, such as viewing the business from the customer's point of view or the "outside-in" and emphasizing broad cross-departmental collaboration at several levels. Next, the key aspects of practices involved in operational leadership are addressed, such as creating a compelling case for change, taking action, and installing accountability for continuous improvement. An overview of major pitfalls in operational leadership is also presented, including topics such as putting methods before outcomes and placing structure before process.

Chapter 3 examines in more detail the practice of crafting and communicating a compelling case for change. Topics examined in this chapter include strategic alignment, developing a shared understanding of the scope of the challenge, and broadly communicating the why, what, and how of operational improvement. Examples of strategic alignment and measuring performance from the customer's point of view are presented.

Chapter 4 takes a more comprehensive treatment of taking action in leading operational improvement. It provides readers with a brief comparison of various improvement methods. It examines key aspects of taking improvement action in various parts of the value chain such as developing new products or services, responding to requests for proposals and fulfilling orders. It proposes that viewing the business in terms of capabilities, or end-to-end processes, is needed for success in operational leadership. An organization's capabilities are defined as those sets of activities that create value for customers, involve significant discretionary costs, can be counted on one or two hands, and almost always require collaboration across two or more departments. The importance of key operational leadership skills, such as pacing and the ability to think at the right level, are emphasized. Some of the common obstacles to success with selected improvement methods are compared. Key questions that leaders need to ask at each major stage of an operational improvement project is outlined and major pitfalls to avoid are enumerated.

Chapter 5 tackles the substantial topic of sustaining improvements to operation performance. Here, the major elements of sustaining change are outlined, including common goals, cross-functional commitment, continuing communication, and celebration. The set of practices needed for change to be deeply embedded in the organization are outlined. Also, this chapter presents the DIRECT model of the personal characteristics of operational leaders, including the being disciplined, inspirational, realistic, enthusiastic, collaborative, and thorough. This model demonstrates that operational leadership can enable greater focus and agility.

Chapter 6 summarizes key concepts for operational leadership in the future and examines topics such as making sense of the glut of management advice from thought leaders; coming to terms with the linkage of strategy and execution; organizing various improvement methods under an umbrella program; crafting a close, collaborative relationship with the leaders in IT; and developing a set of the appropriate leadership mindset and behaviors needed for success.

CHAPTER 2

Principles, Practices, and Pitfalls

As in many other areas of business, success in improving operational performance is a combination of attitude and aptitude. Operational leadership equally relies on a set of principles that form a mindset for change and a set of practices that enable such changes to be executed. The relevant principles are derived, in general, from the body of knowledge on leadership and tailored to the task of improving operational performance. The relevant practices are derived from selected aspects of the body of knowledge on various improvement methods, such as Total Quality Management (TQM), Six Sigma, Lean, Reengineering, and Process Management, and are tailored to the task of improving operational performance in a value-chain context.

There is a substantial body of knowledge on leadership. John P. Kotter's 1996 book *Leading Change* is considered by many to be the seminal work on leading transformational change in how business is conducted to cope with a more challenging business environment. Kotter's eight-step program for leading change[1] applies to a number of major change initiatives, such as downsizing, rightsizing, reengineering, and restructuring.

Kotter's eight-step change theory consists of the following:

1. Establish a sense of urgency.
2. Create a guiding coalition.
3. Develop a vision and a strategy.
4. Communicate the change vision.
5. Empower employees for broad-based action.
6. Generate short-term wins.
7. Consolidate gains and produce more change.
8. Anchor new approaches in the culture.

In contrast to Kotter's work, which targets transformational change, James M. Kouzes and Barry Z. Posner's book—*The Leadership Challenge*—is a practical handbook on leadership skills for individuals. Originally published in 1987, and now in its 4th edition, it offers advice to corporate leaders, entrepreneurs, managers and employees, in both the public and private sectors. In *The Leadership Challenge*, the authors identify five fundamental practices of exemplary leadership:

- Model the way.
- Inspire a shared vision.
- Challenge the process.
- Enable others to act.
- Encourage the heart.

Both of these excellent books on leadership are recommended required reading for leaders faced with improving performance. However, there are some subtle, but important, differences in transforming operations. First, operational leadership applies more frequently to the divisional, regional, or strategic business unit (SBU) level than to an entire corporate organization. Next, it is equally about creating greater value for customers as it is about reducing costs. Finally, a focus is needed on both short-term improvement and long-term sustainability.

There are certain principles that, in combination, represent the mindset of operational leadership. These include the following:

- adopting a value chain perspective of organizational capabilities;
- viewing and measuring business performance from the customers' point of view (the "outside-in"); and
- emphasizing broad cross-departmental collaboration at several levels.

Thinking in terms of organizational capabilities is perhaps the best way to establish a value-chain-based context. An organization's capabilities, or end-to-end processes, if you will, are those sets of activities that create value for customers, involve significant discretionary costs, can be counted on two hands, and almost always require collaboration across two or more departments.[2]

The principle of viewing the business from the customer's point of view is less critical in leading change initiatives such as downsizing and restructuring. These are almost always executed from the top down. In contrast, adopting a value-chain perspective is essential for context and measurement in operational improvement.

Engaging broad cross-functional collaboration is more crucial today than ever before for both the effective improvement of key capabilities and sustaining changes. Decades ago, it was easier to improve operational performance. In those days, the functional areas of research and development (R&D), sales, production, and operations held within their boundaries the key activities needed to develop, sell, make, and deliver products and services. That's no longer the case. Each and every major component of the value chain requires that several departments collaborate. Also, the evolution of marketing as a discipline, the Internet, CRM, and ERP systems has contributed to higher levels of interdependence.[3] Accordingly, the role of IT is now fundamental in enabling dramatic improvements in operational performance. In this day and age, practically any broad-based improvement effort relies extensively on IT. According to Bill Gates, "The first rule of any technology used in a business is that automation applied to an efficient operation will magnify the efficiency. The second is that automation applied to an inefficient operation will magnify the inefficiency."

When the principles of viewing the company in a value chain context and emphasizing collaboration across departments become part of the organizational fabric, the following key practices of operational leadership are more likely to be put into action:

- Create a compelling case for change.
- Take action, execute improvements, think at the right level of detail, and create early wins.
- Assure a tight linkage to information systems.
- Install the infrastructure for continuous improvement.

The practice of improving operational performance relies on improvement methods, and there are common themes among TQM, Six Sigma, and Reengineering. TQM evolved from the work of Dr. W. Edwards Deming on the Plan-Do-Check-Act (PDCA) cycle around a half-century ago. These roots are also evident in the Six Sigma improvement method of Define-Measure-Analyze-Improve-Control (DMAIC). Dr. Michael Hammer, the principal proponent of Reengineering, defined the method of Scoping-Organizing-Redesigning-Implementing.[4] There is a regular dialogue on the misleading "either-or" proposition concerning whether we should engage in incremental or radical improvements in operations. There is no stock answer to this question, as it depends on the needed scope of change and the ability of the organization to absorb that change. Dramatic change is often needed to execute significant operational improvement, *and* incremental continuous improvement is needed to optimize and sustain changes.

The Practices

The practices of operational improvement, which must be led, essentially break down into three core activities: getting ready, taking action, and sustaining gains. In getting ready, the leader needs to create and communicate a compelling case for change and orchestrate the deep commitment of people at various levels and in various departments such that action can be taken. In taking action, the leader needs to encourage the right level of thinking, assure a tight linkage to IT, and assure that there is an iterative method of improvement that produces early wins to maintain momentum. In sustaining gains, the leader's focus is on installing the appropriate measures of operational performance and the infrastructure to institutionalize new behaviors and accountability for continuous improvement.

Creating a compelling case for change is the foundational first step in operational improvement. A compelling case for change is typically built on either an imminent threat or a perceived major opportunity. Either we must join forces and change how we do things to survive, or we must join forces and change how we do things in order to prosper. In some instances, there is a real threat, such as loss of product leadership or shrinking margins. In other situations, a story can be woven to create a threat, such as growth is flattening, and we must do something different right away. The best test of a compelling case for change is whether people step forward as willing followers and whether they are motivated to act with urgency. Executives, middle managers, and frontline employees need to understand the point of change and also agree with it. That's why the case for change needs to tell a compelling story that speaks both to the head and the heart. This is where viewing operations from the customer's point of view becomes important. Many companies do not measure the performance factors that are truly important to the customer, such as delivery of the product or service on time, complete, and error-free. In building a compelling case for change, highlighting the gap between current and desired performance for customers can be a powerful way to touch people's emotions.

Consider the case of a division general manager at a mobile-phone manufacturing company that had experienced a recent loss of market share due to delays in introducing new products. He knew that the company had to compress the cycle time for new product introductions, as that was critical in being first to market and would also drive out cost from the product development process. That point would strike home with logic. But to involve people's emotions, it was important to look at new product development from a customer's point of view. In this respect, what was important to customers was for the division to meet its promised launch dates and introduce products that met customers' expectations in terms of features and functionality. A quick review of performance in meeting promised launch dates over the past 3 years revealed that the dates had been missed nearly 50% of the time. The divisional general manager then had the ingredients for a compelling case for change. He outlined the threat of declining market share and crafted a vision for the future that was based on both speed to market and meeting or exceeding customers' expectations. He sought out and obtained the support of the heads of the R&D, marketing, and sales departments and engaged in dialogue with them to achieve a consensus on goals and targets. Using a variety of means, he then broadly communicated the vision and goals to the entire organization. He challenged employees to deliver products that fulfilled customers' expectations regarding functionality and reliability, speaking to the pride that his people had in their own work and focusing on the importance of keeping promises.

This divisional general manager's success in building a compelling case for change was based on several factors. First, he addressed both the heads and the hearts of his people. Next, he put why and what before who and how. Finally, he invested energy in the broad communication of the shared vision and goals.

Once a compelling case for change has been crafted and communicated, it will go a long way toward assuring that the needed senior-level support for the selected operational improvement initiative will be in place. The practice of taking action, in an iterative way, to improve operational performance applies regardless of the selected method of improvement, be it Lean, Six Sigma, Reengineering, or even a technology-led approach such as deployment of a Business Process Management System (BPMS). The primary requirement for an iterative approach is to define the end-to-end set of activities or process in question, model it at a high level, and for the group of senior managers whose departments are touched by these activities, to be engaged in identifying the key areas for focused project action and potential early wins. While this appears to be straightforward, it can be challenging if some members of the senior group dive into too much detail and have difficulty staying at the right level. This iterative approach can be useful in addressing most operational challenges, including, but not limited to, those related to new product introduction, acquiring and retaining customers, order fulfillment, billing, and responding to customer inquiries. Assuming competent facilitation of the selected improvement methods, the subsequent role of operational leadership in taking action is primarily around pacing, removing obstacles to change, and providing constructive guidance to the project team(s).

The right pacing is essential. Operational leaders must assure that project teams do not dive into too much detail in the early stages of an improvement project in terms of the time and effort needed for modeling and measurement. Similarly, operational leaders look for ways to maintain momentum by way of early wins. These potential early wins are typically related to revising outdated policies and eliminating obviously non-value-added activities and hand-offs. Generally, early wins can be implemented in a month or less and do not require IT investments. Given that major change can take a year or longer, especially if IT is involved in some significant way, planning for and taking action to assure early wins is one of the most important ways to maintain momentum, as the following example on revising an outdated policy illustrates.

Custom Core Products (CCP), a leading technology-component manufacturing company, recognized the need to improve its on-time delivery performance after having conducted a customer survey. CCP's technically advanced products had a dominant position in its markets for years. However, CCP had encountered significant competition in the past two years as competitors introduced products with similar capabilities, albeit slightly lower quality, at a slightly lower price. The result had been a gradual decline in market share over the past 2 years.

Accordingly, CCP conducted a customer survey, which identified a number of areas for improvement. One of the key findings of this survey was that customers believed it took too long to get their orders, and they often received the wrong product. Betty, CCP's Vice President of Administration, which included the Call Center, Finance, Human Resources, and Information Systems, crafted a case for change based on delivering "perfect orders." Perfect orders were defined as orders that were delivered when the customer asked for them, complete (i.e., no backorders) and defect-free. Betty knew that a range of operational improvements were needed to stop the erosion in share of market, but the top priority for CCP was clearly to improve order-delivery performance. Once Betty gained the support of her peers in Sales, Production, and Procurement, she engaged an internal consultant to examine the process from order placed to order delivered and to develop a high-level schematic to review with the members of the leadership team and their relevant direct reports.

The high-level review of the order fulfillment process identified a number of opportunities for improvement, including order accuracy information, credit checking, delays in getting order information to procurement and production scheduling, and improving outbound logistics. The revision of an outdated policy on CCP's credit-checking policy represented an immediate early win opportunity. The current policy was to check credit on every order regardless of the payment history of the customer. Order details were not released to production and procurement until the order had been approved for credit by the finance department. At certain times during the month, this caused delays.

With a stroke of the pen, it was possible to revise the policy on credit checking to automatically approve orders from existing customers with good credit history. Not only did this eliminate non-value-added work and improve workflow, it also constituted an early win that could be communicated to maintain engagement and momentum.

Removing obstacles to change also needs to be front and center on the operational leader's radar. These obstacles can occur at any stage in taking action, but there are typically clear warning signs, such as executives failing to show up for steering-team meetings and project team members failing to actively participate in improvement meetings. Rapid, decisive action in removing obstacles as they are identified is an essential skill set of operational leadership.

Asking thought-provoking questions and providing constructive guidance to the project team(s) tasked with improvement action is another important role of the operational leader. For example, once the project team is ready to present recommendations for improvement, the role of the operational leader is to make sure that the set of recommendations include the following key components:

- a schematic or map of the way in which business should be conducted in the future to achieve goals;
- a succinct matrix of performance measures that should be monitored in the future;
- a concise set of recommendations that captures the rationale for making the contemplated changes to achieve goals supported by a solid business case;
- a high level role-responsibility matrix that details who needs to do what in the future; and
- a high-level implementation plan that indicates who will need to do what by when to implement the recommended actions, with approximate milestones.

If any of these elements are missing or incomplete, or if the pacing is such that it may compromise success, the operational leader needs to ask probing questions and provide constructive guidance. Failure to do so may have significant adverse impacts.

Further details on creating a compelling case for change, taking action, and sustaining gains are presented in chapters 3, 4, and 5, respectively.

The Pitfalls

There are many potential pitfalls in leading substantial change in operational performance. Failing to have a compelling case for change, not engaging the heads of the key departments needed to support the change effort, failing to use a range of media to broadly communicate why the change is needed and the approach to be taken, diving into too much detail too soon and failing to have early wins to demonstrate progress, failing to promptly remove obstacles to change, not installing the right set of metrics, and not building aligned reward and recognition systems to sustain the change are just a few of the major pitfalls.

The following are arguably the most critical to avoid in the early stages of improvement projects:

- a fragile case for change;
- methods before outcomes; and
- structure before workflow.

Given that people in different departments need to collaborate in order to execute improvements in operational performance, a robust case for change is indispensable. Both short-term success and the sustainability of change are threatened whenever the case for change is fragile or weak. What constitutes a fragile case for change? It occurs whenever one or more of the following conditions exist:

- The reason for change is unclear.
- The scope of change needed is unclear.
- The basis for the needed change in operations does not address both the heads and hearts of executives, managers, and the front line.
- There is insufficient communication of the need for change.

The impact of a fragile case for change sometimes becomes evident early, as people actively question the value of the initiative. In other instances, it becomes evident as executives do not attend important meetings or managers fail to appoint the needed resources for the improvement effort, as the following brief example illustrates.

> Greg, the Vice President, Operations in the mortgage division of a national bank (MDNB) was concerned about the cost of processing mortgages. He knew that his people sometimes received mortgages with incomplete or inaccurate information from sales or origination groups, leading to non-value-added work, and that the average cost of processing mortgages was higher than that of some competitors. Greg's case for change was based on becoming the best low-cost processor of mortgages in the industry. At first, he was able to engage his peers in Sales, Underwriting, and IT.
>
> On the surface, his peers seemed to agree with the importance of improving how MDNB processed mortgages. However, as the initiative proceeded, it became increasingly apparent that the needed resources from other departments were not being made available. When Greg confronted his peers with the lack of engagement, they told him, "We know this is important to you, but we have our own priorities."
>
> The cost reduction initiative did produce some results, as some non-value-added activities were eliminated inside operations. But the end-to-end view from application to funding was missing, and overall results were suboptimal.

Greg's case for change was fragile. It failed to speak to the hearts of people in other departments. It failed to give them a reason why they should invest time and resources, and the customer view was absent. The overall initiative would have benefited if Greg's case for change had included the customer view and emphasized the need for speed and accuracy in processing mortgages and funding approved mortgages completely and on time. Other departments in MDNA may have responded more fully if it was not just a matter of reducing costs in the operations department, but was also improving the overall customer experience and making employee work experiences more rewarding.

Emphasizing methods before, or more, than outcomes is another major pitfall to avoid in crafting a case for change in transforming operations. This pitfall occurs whenever a selected method of improving or transforming operations takes on an identity of its own and overshadows the desired outcomes for customers and shareholders. This can happen with any codified improvement method, such as Six Sigma, Lean Six Sigma, or Reengineering. Since most improvement methods require a shift in leadership mindset from a traditional view to a customer-focused, value-chain point of view, it's understandable that there is a certain amount of fanaticism and proselytizing involved. However, it is problematic when the selected method of improvement takes on a life of its own and overshadows the underlying reasons for engaging in fundamental change. Consider the following example.

> Bob was the vice president of quality for a national specialty chemical company (NSC), and an ardent advocate of Six Sigma. Bob's group had established that most of NSC's core operations had sigma levels of 4, at best, and that meant around 6,000 defects per million opportunities. So there was significant potential to reduce defects, reduce costs, and improve the customer experience. NSC had realized a modicum of success with TQM, and Bob convinced the CEO and key members of the leadership team that Six Sigma would take NSC to the next level of performance.
>
> The Six Sigma program was launched with a great deal of fanfare. The CEO emphasized the importance of Six Sigma at town hall meetings in terms of delivering perfect orders to customers and providing world-class customer service. Outside experts were brought in to tell their success with Six Sigma in other companies. A consulting company was engaged to conduct "champion training" for executives and to train a number of high-potential middle managers as Six Sigma Black Belts. Additional Black Belts were hired from the outside.
>
> Within 6 months of the launch of the Six Sigma program, Black Belts had been assigned to each functional area in the organization and assigned the task of delivering three projects per year, where each project would save NSC at least $200,000.00. The bonus compensation of the Black Belts was directly linked to

realizing the targeted cost savings. Hundreds of Green Belts were trained, and dozens of projects were launched. Over time, the focus on cost reduction, by way of individual Six Sigma projects, took precedence over delivering perfect orders to customers and providing world-class customer service, which were the original reasons for launching the program. Two years after the launch of Six Sigma, NSC's margins, or net profit, had only improved slightly when expressed as a percent of sales. Further, the annual customer satisfaction survey, conducted by an outside agency on behalf of NSC, revealed only marginal improvement in customer satisfaction. However, Black Belts had generally hit their targets and had often collected their bonuses. They did so by scoping the Six Sigma projects in such as way as to optimize the chances of success in cost savings and minimize the need for cross-functional collaboration.

NSC continued with the Six Sigma program, but the level of executive attention gradually declined. Then, high-potential Black Belts were assigned to key management positions as these became available, and eventually the remaining Black Belts were left behind in the Quality department, from where they served the needs of various functional areas. Bob became active in exploring the value of Lean to supplement Six Sigma.

In this example, Bob put methods before outcomes. His passion and zeal for the Six Sigma method overshadowed the real reasons for transforming operational performance—delivering orders on time, complete, and defect-free, as well as responding to customer inquiries and complaints right the first time. The selected method of deployment was such that the major workflows that crossed departmental boundaries were never fully examined, and the big improvement opportunities were missed. The pitfall of putting methods before outcomes can occur with virtually any improvement method—be it Lean, Reengineering, or Six Sigma—and with new IT tools or technologies.

The special case of IT tools or technologies being put ahead of desired results or outcomes merits particular attention. Putting methods or tools before outcomes can occur when an information technology solution, such as an ERP or CRM system, is implemented as a bolt-on solution to problems that are not fully defined or understood. ERP horror stories are more common than they should be, involving well-respected organizations such as Goodyear, NASA, and Hershey Foods.[5] Nor is this phenomenon limited to ERP and CRM implementations. Part of the problem is the way in which IT systems have evolved over time. Department heads have insisted that IT systems be developed for use by their function, without adequate consideration of end-to-end workflows and the related operational factors. In larger companies, mergers and acquisitions have necessitated that the IT department cobble together systems that were not designed to be compatible. The resulting IT environment is frequently characterized by interfaces that were custom-designed, require continuing attention, and are expensive to maintain. No wonder that companies spend over 80% of their IT budget dedicated to "keeping the lights on."[6] In spite of this history, companies persist in their search of the "silver bullet," and when they think they've found it, place tools before outcomes or results.

Putting structure before workflow is yet another major pitfall to avoid in leading operational change. This practice flies in the face of the long-held dictum that form follows function—in other words, an understanding of workflow will reveal insights that are useful in determining organization design. While some degree of restructuring may be involved in transforming operations, it is best done after workflow considerations are understood and in a phased method. The wholesale restructuring of the organization chart, in advance of understanding the end-to-end business processes that create value for customers, has the tendency to motivate people, somewhat naturally, to focus more on personal relationships versus performing for customers.

Lucy was the Chief Operating Officer of a national property and casualty insurance company (PCIC). An avid student of management practices, Lucy became convinced that the concept of "getting the right people on the bus" was needed at PCIC. Lucy knew that there were a number of major operational challenges to be overcome if PCIC was to enjoy continuing profitable growth. Customers were dissatisfied with the timeliness of claims processed by PCIC. New service introduction lagged behind the competition and PCIC was rarely first to market with new service offerings.

Lucy succeeded in convincing PCIC's CEO that a wholesale change in organization structure was needed. The CEO and COO worked together with an outside consultant to develop a plan where sales districts were reorganized, regional claims processing units were consolidated, and back-office functions centralized in a new shared services organization. Lucy believed that once the right people were in place, PCIC would be well positioned to address and overcome the key operational challenges. It was expected that some time would be needed for people to become accustomed to the new organization structure, and that indeed turned out to be the case. People needed time to become familiar with new reporting structures and build new relationships. As the restructuring took place, new, more pressing issues were identified and the original intent of focusing on excellence in claims processing and new service introduction took a back seat to other priorities.

Lucy put structure before outcomes. Her passion for getting the right boxes on the organization chart and the "right people on the bus" distracted the organization from the real reasons for transforming operational performance: processing claims on time and introducing new services faster and better and right the first time. As the major workflows that crossed departmental boundaries in claims processing and new service introduction were not fully examined and documented prior to the restructuring, there was no enduring context established for taking action on major improvement opportunities.

The principles outlined in this chapter can assist leaders in avoiding the pitfalls of making a fragile case for change, putting methods before outcomes, and placing structure before workflow. The ability to view the business from the customer's point of view, and measure current performance in this respect, is particularly critical. One additional element to note is the ability to think at the right level of detail. Representing operational performance at a high level supported with a one-page, visually compelling schematic provides the means for asking key questions around performance and for engaging other leaders. This is far superior to diving into a great deal of detail, be it with a cluttered value-stream map or a confusing process relationship map. When too much detail is introduced too early in launching improvement projects, people understandably react with comments such as, "Let's not boil the ocean" and "This seems just too hard, let's reduce the scope." Yet, what is actually needed for optimal results is the big-picture view where customers come first in establishing context for any dramatic improvements in operational performance.

Several of the major pitfalls in leading operational improvements are related to actions in the early stages of initiatives. However, even when operational improvements are launched effectively, they can go off the rails when early wins are not captured to maintain momentum, when management attention drifts, when the needed collaboration with IT is absent, or when there is not ongoing infrastructure for sustaining changes.

Table 2.1 outlines some of the major pitfalls for operational leaders to note and to address in taking action and sustaining changes.

Additional details on creating a compelling case for change, taking action, and sustaining gains are presented in Chapters 3, 4, and 5, respectively.

Table 2.1. Pitfalls to Avoid in Taking Action and Sustaining Change

Pitfalls to avoid in taking action	Pitfalls to avoid in sustaining change
Pacing is too slow. The team becomes bogged down in analysis, measurement, or both.	The new, recommended performance measures are not incorporated into the senior leadership team's scorecard.
Obstacles to change are identified, but prompt action is not taken to remove these.	The recommended alignment of recognition and rewards is delayed or forgotten.
Momentum continues in spite of a weak business case.	Declaring victory before the new work practices become "the way we do things around here."[7]
IT involvement is late or inconsistent, and the recommended IT enhancements are low on the project priority list.	Shifting priorities lead to a decrease in continuing management attention.
HR involvement is late or inconsistent, and the recommended training is low on the HR project priority list.	There is insufficient effort invested in establishing the infrastructure for continuous improvement.

Chapter Summary

There exists excellent literature on leading change, which is recommended required reading for leaders faced with improving performance. However, there are some subtle, but important, differences in transforming operations that call for a different viewpoint.

Viewing the business from the customers' point of view, adopting a value-chain perspective of organizational capabilities, emphasizing broad cross-departmental collaboration at several levels, and focusing on both short-term improvement and long-term sustainability are some of the key principles in leading operational improvements.

Building a compelling case for change involves addressing both people's emotions and logic, putting why and what before how, and investing substantial energy in the broad communication of shared vision and goals.

Leaders need to avoid the pitfalls of a fragile case for change, such as putting methods before outcomes and placing structure before workflow. A fragile case for change exists whenever the reason for change is unclear, the scope of change needed is unclear, the basis for the needed change in operations does not address both the heads and hearts of executives and managers, or there is insufficient communication of the need for change. The abilities to view the business from the customer's point of view, to measure current performance, and to think at the right level of detail are critical in this respect.

Even when operational improvements are launched effectively, they can go off the rails when early wins are not captured to maintain momentum, when management attention drifts, and when the needed collaboration with IT is absent.

A number of examples were presented to illustrate the major pitfalls of making a weak case for change, putting methods before outcomes, and placing structure before results.

CHAPTER 3

A Compelling
Case for Change

The likelihood of success in any significant improvement of operational performance is low unless the leader crafts a compelling case for change. There are simply too many people, too many departments, and too many competing initiatives involved. A compelling case for change must be aligned with strategy. It must address the why and what of the needed improvement in operational performance and provide both logical and emotional reasons for people to be wholeheartedly committed to a common course of action.

Strategic Alignment

Aligning major operational improvement initiatives with strategy is a prerequisite for success. Fortunately, there are only a finite number of strategic options. The challenge for most organizations is to choose a strategic position and take action to implement it. In *Competitive Strategy*, considered by many to be *the* classic treatment of strategic options, Porter argued that firms must decide to pursue a strategy that is based either on cost leadership, differentiation, or focus.[1] Firms that are unable to choose, focus, and execute are subject to being "stuck in the middle," will not likely enjoy competitive advantage, and may become targets for mergers and acquisitions. While strategy is typically determined in the head office, it must be executed at the business unit or division level, and the implementation of strategy invariably requires broad cross-functional collaboration in improving the set of value-creating activities. Accordingly, Porter cautioned that "left to its own devices, each functional department will inevitably pursue approaches dictated by its professional orientation and the incentives of those in charge."[2]

Treacy and Wiersema outlined three customer-value propositions, closely aligned with the aforementioned strategic options: operational excellence, customer intimacy, and product leadership.[3] They also proposed that firms must excel at one of these strategic options AND perform at least at industry standard in the other two to become market leaders.

In a phrase, "strategy is choosing what game to play," and operational improvement represents how best to play the game. A company must deliver greater value to customers, create comparable value at a lower cost, or do both. Doing so requires an understanding of the value-creating activities that are the basic units of competitive advantage. Porter emphasized that "overall advantage or disadvantage results from all a company's activities, not only a few. Ultimately, all differences between companies in cost or price derive from the hundreds of activities required to create, produce, sell, and deliver their products or services, such as calling on customers, assembling final products, and training employees."[4] Table 3.1 compares generic strategies to value disciplines.

Table 3.1. Comparison of Generic Strategies to Value Disciplines

Generic strategies (Porter)		Value disciplines (Treacy & Wiersema)	
Cost leadership	Be the low-cost producer in an industry for a given level of quality.	Operational excellence	Lead in price and convenience and optimize business processes across functional and organizational boundaries.
Differentiation	Develop a product or service that offers unique attributes that are valued by customers and that customers perceive to be better than, or different from, the products of the competition.	Customer intimacy	Tailor and shape products and services to fit an increasingly fine definition of the customer.
Focus	Concentrate on a narrow segment, and within that segment, attempt to achieve either a cost advantage or differentiation.	Product leadership	Produce a continuous stream of state-of-the-art products and services.

Once a strategic position has been selected, the role of operational leadership is to take focused action in improving operational performance.

Those organizations that elect to pursue a cost leadership strategy, which is sometimes referred to as low-cost or an operational excellence value discipline, generally need to address some or all of the following:[5]

- an emphasis on excellence in manufacturing process engineering to eliminate intermediate production steps;
- review of operations to minimize overhead costs, reduce transaction costs;
- order fulfillment that works to deliver products or services to customers perfectly, at competitive prices, on time, complete, and with zero defects; and
- a robust new product development process in which products are designed for efficient manufacturing.

Organizations that elect to follow a differentiation strategy based on a product leadership value discipline generally need to address some or all of the following:

- excellence in the sales and marketing processes from inquiry to order;
- a new product development process that is engineered for speed; and
- an emphasis on innovation such that they themselves render their own technology obsolete.

Finally, organizations that choose to pursue a focus strategy, which is sometimes referred to as a niche strategy, and is based on a customer-intimacy value discipline, generally need to address some or all of the following:

- tailoring of new product development to suit the evolving needs of a relatively narrow market segment; and
- refinement of processes such as order fulfillment and responding to customer inquiries to build customer loyalty for the long term.

Aligning major operational improvement initiatives with strategy requires that the leader ask and answer the question, "Which of our capabilities, or business processes, need to be improved, by how much, and by when, in order to achieve our strategic objectives?" Sometimes the answer to this question is evident, as the following example illustrates.

The merger had been signed. While regulatory approval had not yet been obtained, the regulatory authorities had provided the go-ahead for the two diversified chemical companies to address supply-chain-related transition issues over the next few months. Rick, the Senior Vice President for Supply Chain of the dominant partner in this merger, knew he would have to act rapidly and decisively to address the broad range of transition issues related to order fulfillment that included items such as inventory relabeling, permits and registrations, and the revision of countless electronic and printed documents. It was clear that both companies pursued a cost leadership strategy and that this would continue to be the strategic position of the merged entity.

The premerger activities would need to focus on order fulfillment, and it would only be postmerger that other related processes such as procurement and production would be improved in the merged company. The systems issues were daunting. Rick had heard the horror stories of other mergers failing to meet shareholder expectations. Indeed, only about a third of mergers were reported to have met the original expectation. One case that stuck in his mind was that of the Union Pacific (UP) and Southern Pacific (SP), where, after the merger, rail traffic logjams, lost railcars, and train delays had become commonplace. The damage to the entire U.S. economy had been estimated at over $2 billion due to the UP-SP merger fiasco, and customers left the new company in droves to find alternative means of shipping their goods. Rick was determined to avoid a similar catastrophe. He knew that the case for change needed to be made first and foremost to the leadership team of both companies. Once he had engaged both leadership teams, he believed he would get the resources needed for success. He crafted three key messages.

The first key message was that on the first day of merged operations, the company would not give any customer a reasonable excuse to go elsewhere. That means that customer orders would be taken, products would be delivered, invoices would be issued, money would be collected, and bills would be paid—and all of this, and more, would be done on time, accurately, and safely.

The second key message was that over 70% of mergers fail to achieve the original objectives and that this is most frequently due to challenges in integrating operations. This message would be reinforced and illustrated with the UP-SP horror story.

The third message was that it would not be easy to optimize supply-chain work processes and the related enabling systems in the next few months such that the new organization would be ready to consummate the merger. But it could be, and would be, done. There were to be no "major" systems changes prior to the actual merger, and change management—as well as disciplined project and program management practices—would be essential to success.

Rick did receive the needed resources, and the premerger activities were carried out successfully such that on the first day of merged operations, all orders were delivered perfectly. The ingredients for success in this example included a clear alignment to strategy (operational excellence), viewing the business from the customer's perspective (order delivery and customer satisfaction), and inspiring people by addressing both facts and feelings (we will not make the same mistakes as others have, and this can and will be done).

In this example, the compelling need to prepare for the integration phase of the merger, the clear alignment to a strategy based on operational excellence, and the decision on which aspect of operational performance to begin with was straightforward. But that's not always the case. The way in which some organizations choose to articulate strategy can make it difficult to align operational improvements with strategy. This occurs when strategy is expressed in very broad terms, such as "becoming a leader in our industry." In such cases, the role of operational leadership is to probe what that means for the firm's major capabilities of developing, selling, making, and delivering its products and services. By so doing, leadership can avoid major pitfalls such as focusing on cost reduction when the thrust of strategy is actually on growth, or vice versa.

Even when the direction of strategic alignment is clear, there are decisions to be made in terms of priorities. Whenever an organization's chosen strategy is based on product leadership, the inclination may be to begin with an assessment of the new product or service process and to make significant improvements to this capability or end-to-end process if needed. Yet, an improvement in the related operational processes in the sales, marketing, and procurement areas may actually represent equal or greater priorities. Whenever the organization's chosen strategy is cost leadership or operational excellence, the inclination may be to begin with an assessment of the order fulfillment process, and make significant improvements to this end-to-end process or capability, if needed. Yet, an improvement in the related operational processes in the customer service and procurement areas may actually represent equal or greater priorities. One of the principal methods of deciding on the sequence of operational improvement activities—and, at the same time, gathering more data to build a compelling case for change—is to examine the current performance of key customer-touching activities from the point of view of the customer. While most organizations have excellent data on cost and volume statistics, data on the quality and timeliness of how the organization is performing for customers is frequently overlooked. Table 3.2 provides insight into the types of current performance metrics, viewed from the perspective of the customer, that can assist leaders in selecting the sequence of improvement priorities and that can also provide more data to build a compelling case for change.

Aligning operational improvement with strategy can also be complicated when some members of the leadership team believe that strategy drives structure. This can lead to premature and frequent revisions of the organization chart. In this instance, the operational leader needs to make a strong case for the interdependence of strategy, structure, process, people, and rewards, and emphasize that *first* taking steps to understand the performance of the firm's capabilities or end-to-end processes can provide important information on potential, future refinements that may be needed in organizational structure and reward systems.[6]

Table 3.2. Measuring Performance From the Customer's Point of View

Capability (activity set, end-to-end process)	Typical metrics meaningful to customers
Service delivery (order to installation)	On time (when promised), accurate, and complete
Order fulfillment (order to delivery)	On time (when promised), accurate, and complete
Billing	User-friendly, accurate, and complete
New product introduction (idea to launch)	On time, meets customers' expectations
Inquiry resolution (inquiry to resolution)	Right the first time, complete
Claim settlement (report to settle)	On time (when promised), accurate, and complete
Service restoration (report to restore)	Fast (when promised), right the first time
Enrollment (application to policy)	On time (when promised), accurate, and complete

The Case for Change

While a compelling case for change does need to be aligned with strategy and address the why and what of the planned improvement in operational performance, it also has to provide both logical and emotional reasons for people to be wholeheartedly committed to a common course of action. In this respect, the factors that motivate employees to act are often different from those that resonate with the members of the senior leadership team. Factors such as growth, profit, and competitive advantage are likely to capture the attention of executives, while other factors such as customer satisfaction and pride in their work may do more to engage employees in the case for change.

Given strategic alignment, the other key considerations in crafting a compelling case for change include

- stating what improvement in operational performance is needed and why;
- addressing both facts and feelings;
- using simple, visually gripping support materials; and
- communicating key messages repeatedly.

Once the case for change has been made, examine the level of urgency. The best test of whether there is a persuasive case for change is whether people are compelled to act. Once in a while, the mandate is clear, as in the case of the merger described earlier. More often, it takes careful thought and effort to align with a strategy and build the case for change. Consider the following example.

> Ray, the Chief Operating Officer of a local operating company (LOC) within a regional electric utility (REU), recognized that the steady deregulation of the electric utility sector called for significant improvements in operational performance. For decades, REU had generated and delivered electricity to customers in their service territories. A few years ago, as part of electric deregulation in their serviced territories, REU and other electric utilities were required to sell their electric generating plants to private firms. As a result, REU no longer produced electricity; instead, it delivered electricity produced by other firms. More deregulation was on the horizon, and Ray was convinced that the best way to keep current customers was to excel at those aspects of operations that were important to customers. Strategy was developed at the REU level. REU's strategy emphasized developing regulated electric and natural gas businesses successfully. That meant finding ways to optimize investments and operations such that each key stakeholder would benefit. At the operating company level, this meant a focus on operational excellence—that much was clear to Ray. He knew that the LOC's customers wanted lower energy prices; however, LOC couldn't do a lot about that. But Ray recognized that improvements were needed to meet customers' expectations in areas such as on-time performance for new installations, reliable delivery of energy, prompt restoration of service in case of an outage, and accurate invoices. The set of core values at REU had been adopted by each of the operating companies and included values such as
>
> • safety first;
> • high ethical standards;
> • superior customer and community service; and
> • environmental stewardship.

In order to develop a compelling case for change, Ray asked a group of analysts to examine the LOC's performance in the areas of new service installation and outage restoration. These factors were within LOC's control, while billing activities were done on a shared service basis within the REU. A rapid examination of current performance for new service installation revealed that there were clear opportunities to improve this activity, especially for new business customers. A key insight was that LOC's current way of measuring new service installation needed revision, from an inside-out perspective to a more customer-focused view. On the other hand, LOC had good data for outage restoration and measured both the System Average Interruption Duration Index (SAIDI) and the Customer Average Interruption Duration Index (CAIDI).

Ray and his direct reports developed two clear objectives for the case for change: improve on-time new service installation by 10% during the current fiscal year and reduce CAIDI by 15% during the same period.

To build the case for why these improvements were essential, Ray relied on emphasizing LOC core values and a recent J. D. Power and Associates report that claimed that "a utility provider that combines value with a solid customer-oriented image is more likely to have a competitive advantage."

The result of this preparation was a brief, high-energy presentation shared with his direct reports and then delivered to staff via a town hall meeting. Ray emphasized three key messages.

The first key message was that the LOC was deeply committed to meeting or exceeding customer expectation in several areas. That meant that customer orders for new service installations would be filled when promised, and any disruptions in service would be restored faster than in prior years—and this would be done accurately and safely.

The second key message was that customer orientation and outstanding service should be considered the pillars of competitive advantage. This message was reinforced and illustrated with excerpts from the J. D. Power report.

The third message was that it would not be easy to optimize work processes, and he called on the professional pride of all LOC employees to work together, live the REU-LOC core values, and collaborate such that the objectives would be accomplished—and accomplished during the current fiscal year.

As the LOC example illustrates, the answers to key questions concerning the feasibility of strategic implementation can be answered only at the operational level. While strategy is the framework of choices that determine the nature and direction of an organization, every strategy must stand up to two reality checks—will it work and can we implement it?[7]

The case for change in implementing an effective business strategy will, at a minimum, answer the following questions:

- How will we win?
- What must we do?
- How will we measure progress?

Acting to assure close collaboration with the information technology (IT) department and the chief information officer (CIO) begins right here. In drafting the case for change, the IT issues may not yet be evident, but, rest assured, they soon will arise.

The case for change has to be specific enough to serve as the foundation for taking action and inspiring enough to generate wide-spread commitment. The best litmus test of the case for change is whether there are willing followers for a commonly understood course of action. The extent to which this exists only becomes clear when people collaborate across traditional organizational boundaries to improve performance.

Chapter Summary

The likelihood of success in any significant improvement of operational performance is low unless the leader crafts a compelling case for change. There are simply too many people, too many departments, and too many competing initiatives involved. Aligning major operational improvement initiatives with strategy is a prerequisite for success. Fortunately, there are only a finite number of strategic options. Once a strategic position has been selected, the role of operational leadership is to take focused action in improving operational performance.

Aligning major operational improvement initiatives with strategy requires that the leader ask and answer the question, "Which of our capabilities or business processes need to be improved, by how much, and by when, in order to achieve our strategic objectives?"

Aligning operational improvement with strategy can also be complicated when some members of the leadership team believe that strategy drives structure and place undue priority on playing with the organization chart, as that is what affects status and power.

A compelling case for change needs to address the why and what of the planned improvement in operational performance, and it has to provide both logical and emotional reasons for people to be wholeheartedly committed to a common course of action. Measuring performance from the customer's point of view can assist in prioritizing improvement opportunities and can provide useful data in building a strong case for change. The factors that motivate broad-based engagement by employees may differ from the factors that capture the attention of the senior leadership team. Other key considerations in crafting a compelling case for change are outlined. Examples demonstrating strategic alignment and building a case for change are presented.

The case for change must answer the questions of "how will we win, what must we do, and how will we measure progress." It has to be specific enough to serve as the foundation for taking action and sufficiently inspiring to generate widespread commitment, as demonstrated by willing followers for a commonly understood course of action.

CHAPTER 4

Leading Operational Improvement

Given a compelling case for change, the challenge is to proactively lead successful major improvements in operational performance and that calls for managing change. The historical odds of success has hovered around 30% in successfully leading major change efforts. This has little to do with a deficit in improvement methods, tools, or even management advice. There are ample improvement methods—the issue is how these improvements are deployed. Nor is there a deficit of increasingly agile technology; again, the issue is one of selection and how the selected technology is deployed. There is also ample management advice available, and the challenge is one of implementation leadership.

In addition to a robust method of improvement, leaders also need a shared understanding of context, the ability to focus on major leverage points, and the means to generate quick wins in order to maintain momentum.

Comparison of Improvement Methods

Most of today's popular improvement methods evolved from the work of W. Edwards Deming, Joseph M. Juran, and the quality movement of the 1970s and 1980s. That is certainly true for Six Sigma, Lean, and Lean Six Sigma. In contrast to the incremental improvement methods spawned from the quality movement, the reengineering method advocated a more radical approach and argued that while incremental improvements were necessary, they were not sufficient for transformational change.[1] Process management evolved as an umbrella approach that emphasized a disciplined method for improving and managing the operational performance of the entire set of a company's end-to-end business processes. There are also a number of specific methods targeting transformation, such as "rapid results" and accelerating corporate transformation.[2] In the interest of brevity, this section offers a concise comparison of Six Sigma, Lean, Reengineering, and Process Management.

Six Sigma, and by extension, Lean Six Sigma, are arguably the methods that are best codified through training and a standardized approach toward operational improvement. While Six Sigma was developed by Motorola in the 1980s, it was popularized by General Electric in the 1990s. Six Sigma is a both a specific measure of quality, namely 3.4 defects per million opportunities, and a structured method of improvement for reducing variation and eliminating defects. The DMAIC method (define-measure-analyze-improve-control) for incremental improvement is in most widespread use, but Six Sigma also includes techniques for more radical change via different versions of DFSS (Design for Six Sigma), such as DMADV (define-measure-analyze-design-verify) and DMEDI (define-measure-explore-develop-implement). In theory, Six Sigma can be deployed at the enterprise level for broad-based improvement. In practice, it is typically deployed on a functional or departmental basis and characterized by a large number of small, nonconnected projects of relatively limited scope. This results from the deployment practice of tasking Six Sigma Black Belts with a target of leading four to six projects per year, where each yields between $150,000 and $500,000 of cost savings. This practice has the effect of creating a bias toward smaller projects, employing an incremental improvement approach, and serving to displace the focus on the customer with a focus on cost reduction.[3]

While Six Sigma continues to be in widespread use in a long list of companies—such as General Electric, Allied Signal, Bank of America, Dow Chemical, Caterpillar, Honeywell, Motorola, DuPont, American Express, Ford, and many others, it is not without its critics.[4] Some have argued that it's a tool that is "very useful for one set of problems, and largely useless for many others," and that it is particularly useful for attacking problems that are "hard to find and easy to fix" and less applicable when a firm is faced with problems relating to some fundamental flaw in organization or workflow design. These more systemic problems were characterized as "easy to find, and hard to fix."[5] Even though a handful of expert training organizations have codified the Six Sigma technique, the degree of customer focus does indeed vary. In one Six Sigma training program rolled out in a billion-dollar company, the customer was not mentioned until page 37 and then not again until page 127 in the training program documentation. Further, the battery of statistical tools in Six Sigma is not only daunting, it has been criticized as excessive, including over three dozen tools, of which no more than a handful are frequently applied.[6] Nevertheless, Six Sigma continues to be widely used as a means to improve operations, as leaders are attracted to the rigor of the method and the comprehensive array of statistical tools.

Lean, which is also known as the Toyota Production System, Lean Manufacturing, and Lean Management System, emphasizes speed, eliminating waste, and creating value for customers through the reduction of non-value-added activities.[7] Lean also has a battery of tools, again mostly derived from the quality movement of the 1970s and 1980s; however, it often relies principally on "value-stream mapping" and "kaizen" projects, as opposed to the statistical approach of Six Sigma. Value-stream mapping is a one-page visual schematic used to identify ways to eliminate waste and non-value-added activities. Kaizen is a focused technique of continuous improvement in the performance of a set of activities, typically of smaller scope. In Lean, there is an emphasis on understanding the current state, the ideal state, and the future state. Further, with Lean, the "respect for people" principle is a key element in achieving long-term success.[8]

The Lean method has also been well documented and is codified due largely to the influence of the Lean Enterprise Institute, Inc. (LEI). There are five lean principles defined by the founder of the Lean Enterprise Institute:

- Provide the value actually desired by customers.
- Identify the value stream for each product.
- Line up the value stream for each product.
- Line up the remaining steps in a continuous flow.
- Let the customer pull value from the firm.

The Lean method has made important advances in the concept of "flow," and the training for Lean is less time-consuming than that needed for Six Sigma. While Lean is still predominantly used in the manufacturing sector, it has made some major strides in the service sector as well.[9]

With Lean, it is often possible to improve operational performance factors, such as product lead times to customers and on-time delivery, the financial benefits may lag operational performance.[10]

Reengineering, introduced by Michael Hammer in the early 1990s, advocates the radical redesign of an organization's large business processes. Unlike incremental improvement methods, which involve the careful planning and execution of improvement in small, cautious steps, the reengineering method contemplates transformational change—an all or nothing proposition.[11] Hammer and Champy defined reengineering as "the *fundamental* rethinking and *radical* redesign of business *processes* to achieve *dramatic* improvements in critical, contemporary measures of performance such as cost, quality, service and speed."[12] The training and documentation for the reengineering method has not been codified to the same extent as other improvement methods, as many consulting companies have their own proprietary method of reengineering. However, reengineering projects generally follow the four major stages of scoping, organizing, redesigning, and implementing.[13] Around the same time as the evolution of reengineering, other approaches—such as Process Innovation—were launched that encompassed "the envisioning of new work strategies, the actual process design activity, and the implementation of the change in all its complex human, organizational and technological dimensions."[14] These various approaches to radical change claimed to embrace both the human side of change and the power of enabling information technology; yet, in practice, "reengineering" often became a buzzword for cost cutting.

Process Management represented a more balanced approach, encompassing both dramatic and incremental improvements in operational performance. Originally outlined by Rummler and Brache in their seminal book *Improving Performance: Managing the White Space on the Organization Chart*, process improvement and management provided guidance on how companies could be organized and managed to produce superior performance.[15] Central to the concept of process management was the premise that an organization operates on three levels—organization, process, and individual performer—and that superior performance demands that a company must put goals and measures, designs, and management practices in place at each level. Over time, process management came to represent a disciplined method to improve and manage the operational performance of the entire set of a company's end-to-end business pro-cesses. Essentially, process management involves the definition of a com-pany's end-to-end processes (typically 5 to 10), measuring performance from both the customer's and the company's points of view, designating process owners with responsibility and accountability for process per-formance, selecting two or three processes for improvement action, and sustaining gains through ongoing management of the firm's end-to-end processes. This cycle should then be repeated until the entire operations of the firm have been optimized.[16]

In recognition of the increasing role of information technol-ogy in enabling operational performance, Business Process Manage-ment (BPM) is an extension of the concepts of process management. BPM has been defined as a deliberate and collaborative approach for systematically—and systemically—managing all of a company's busi-ness processes.[17] BPM is enabled by business-process thinking and process-centric information technologies. Software vendors have devel-oped applications called Business Process Management Suites (BPMS) that generally contain a process engine for addressing workflow issues through modeling and execution, an analytics capability that enables the monitoring and reporting of key metrics, the means to facilitate document control and versioning, and collaboration tools such as por-tals and forums. Given the evolution of disparate information systems, and the difficulty of linking legacy systems, the application of BPMS on a company-wide basis would appear, in theory, to hold significant potential. Yet, in practice, BPM is often applied in solving tactical prob-lems of small scope, and the linkage to other improvement methodolo-gies often does not occur. Both business leaders and senior IT managers are reluctant to tackle the large components of the value-chain or core capabilities, due to the difficulty of linking the BPM tool to the exist-ing IT infrastructure and dealing with the number and complexity of the needed interfaces. As one senior manager at a BPMS software ven-dor stated, "Many of our clients come to us with a pain point in their operations, and they simply want the pain to go away. They are not yet ready to deploy BPM at the enterprise level." Further, the long-stand-ing IT-business divide endures and presents challenges in effective BPM deployment, which requires close IT-business collaboration.

The proliferation of improvement methods over the past two decades with approaches such as Six Sigma, Lean, Lean Six Sigma, Continuous Process Improvement, Reengineering, Process Management, and many others—including Balanced Scorecard and Supply Chain Management—has led many companies to deploy two or more methods in an attempt to wring improved performance from operations. This often leads to multiple disconnected efforts, with each group advocating, with almost religious zeal, that their approach is *the* best way, leading to a competition for resources. The resulting skepticism, and even cynicism, by employees is understandable, as there is often a lack of clarity regarding how these programs relate to one another. To illustrate one flagrant example, at one insurance company, there were teams concurrently working on the "voice of the customer," balanced scorecard, and reengineering. Each team had time on the agenda of the executive group, and yet the teams rarely communicated with one another.

The launch of the currently popular improvement methods is typically accompanied by a great deal of fanfare and hoopla. Programs typically start off well, generate excitement, show promising early signs of progress, and yet often fail to produce planned results. Indeed, studies suggest that around 60% of corporate Six Sigma programs fail to generate desired results,[18] and nearly 70% of reengineering efforts have been widely reported to fail. Similarly, while thousands of companies have launched Lean programs, most have achieved only modest levels of improvement, typically in only one part of the business, such as operations. A survey by the Lean Enterprise Institute, Inc., reported that only 4% of respondents characterized their progress with Lean as "advanced."[19]

The Challenge of Leading Operational Improvements

What's the problem? Why are the results so unimpressive? A comparison of the obstacles to success with Six Sigma and Lean, presented in Table 4.1, indicates some common themes.

When it comes to transformation, leaders make things too complex. They have multiple teams working on tactical issues, and these efforts sometimes overlap. They clutter the landscape with jargon. They hire too many consultants and chase too many fads.[22]

Table 4.1. Obstacles to Success with Six Sigma and Lean

Six Sigma[20]	Lean[21]
Often deployed with a functional, departmental bias	Lack of a sense of urgency
Too many small and disconnected projects	Backsliding to old ways of working
Overreliance on Black Belts	Resistance by middle managers
Suboptimal linkage to the use of enabling technology	Regarding Lean as the "flavor of the month"
Lack of implementation know-how	Failing to remove obstacles to change
Lack of sustained senior management participation	Lack of implementation know-how
Lip service to customer focus, but the real emphasis is on cost reduction	Lack of sustained senior management participation
	Lack of customer focus

The truth is that most organizations struggle with complexity, especially now in the age of global supply chains and markets, increasing regulation, technological disruption, and communications overload. Further, the way leaders elect to manage organizations—typically characterized by frequent reorganizations, the proliferation of product and service offerings, and the number of time-wasting meetings and non-value-added management activities—unnecessarily adds to the level of complexity.[23]

Leaders also struggle with jargon and chase too many fads. Part of the reason for the failure of operational improvement initiatives is that in the rush to change their organizations, executives end up immersing their companies in an alphabet soup of initiatives.[24] This is in spite of the fact that most improvement methods share very similar common steps. Once a case for change has been made, most methods involve four generic stages: definition, analysis, design, and implementation. The definition stage, sometimes called "getting ready," "scoping," or "chartering," involves the establishment of the project scope, goals, and schedule. The analysis phase, sometimes called "understanding the current state" or "as-is," involves an assessment of current work practices for the selected scope and identification of disconnects, problems, issues, and opportunities. The design stage involves taking action to eliminate problems and capitalize on opportunities, and the implementation stage involves taking action to realize the desired "to be" or future state. Don't leaders recognize the striking similarity across various improvement methods? If they did, then they would not launch concurrent, and sometimes competing, initiatives. Don't they understand that they have key roles to play in each stage? If they did, then the obstacles outlined in Table 4.1 would be less pervasive.

Many executives don't appear to understand that there are key leverage points for each capability, such as developing and introducing new products, acquiring and retain customers, fulfilling orders, and so on. The "stage-gate" concept of new product development, defined nearly two decades ago, provides insight into the key leverage points in this capability.[25] These key leverage points in new product development include a continuing focus on customer involvement throughout, making it front-end loaded (due diligence at the business-case stage), and employing cross-functional teams.[26] The customer acquisition capability, in the context of manufacturing companies, invariably involves leveraging key activities in following up leads and responding to requests for proposals (RFPs). The key leverage point for fulfilling orders invariably involves order accuracy and setting the promise date for delivery or installation. These leverage points exist for nearly every capability in most industries—manufacturing, banking, insurance, health care, and even government. Yet, companies often fail to focus on these areas and persist in rediscovery.

Another part of the problem is that while each of the improvement methods compared above has documented training for working team members, there is far less guidance, especially at the practical level, available to senior managers. In part, this may be a result of the fact that much of the training material used in the popular improvement methods is produced by subject-matter experts who have little direct executive managerial experience. So it's not surprising that leaders don't understand that you can't "PowerPoint" your way to success.[27] They often do not appreciate the importance of their roles in getting ready, pacing, assuring momentum by rapidly capturing quick wins, constructively challenging the designs and plans of the working team, and assuring that the needed elements are in place for implementation success. The ability to think at the right level of detail is one of the critical success factors in this respect. This means exercising discipline at the getting-ready stage to think at a high level, avoid diving into too much detail too soon, and assuring that the customer's perspective is considered. Here, as opposed to coming up with solutions, the leader's emphasis should be on seeking to understand and on asking probing questions. In contrast, at the taking-action stage, it is important for senior managers to think at a more granular level of detail, encourage the prioritization of the opportunities for improvement, and push for the rapid implementation of the so-called early wins that can be implemented in less than 30 days, in order to demonstrate progress and maintain momentum. The role of senior managers is to provide guidance and feedback at each stage of an improvement project.

The getting-ready phase involves the establishment of the project scope, goals, schedule, and constraints. The role of the leader is to ensure that

- the goals from the case for change are shared and communicated;
- the selected scope is broad enough to assure the results;
- the needed cross-functional collaboration at both management and working team levels is in place;
- the schedule is aggressive yet achievable; and
- the downstream impact of any constraints is fully understood.

Each of these activities can be challenging. Leading operational improvement requires not only that the goals be clear and shared but also that these goals embrace both the customer experience and company requirements. Further, the selected scope must be broad enough and demand cross-departmental collaboration, as the largest opportunities for performance improvement occur at cross-departmental hand-offs. In the mortgage division of a national bank (MDNA) example presented in chapter 2, the vice president of operations committed several cardinal sins. Not only was his case for change weak, as it did not represent the customer view, he was also mostly interested in reducing the cost of processing mortgages in his own department and did not realize that the lack of accuracy and completeness of mortgage applications received from the origination department had a material impact on the amount of rework and non-value-added activities in his own department. Nor did he appreciate that the policies and activities in the underwriting would have a material impact on the overall cycle time to process mortgages. In the absence of collaboration with these departments, it's not surprising that the improvement results turned out to be suboptimal.

In the getting ready stage, it's also important to acquire an appreciation for potential issues around constraints. The following example illustrates the failure to appreciate the downstream impact of constraints.

Gary was the General Manager of Corporate Operations for the Caribbean Regional Bank (CRB). CRB recognized the importance of excelling in processing personal loans as one of the keys to success in maintaining and extending its competitive advantage in its retail banking line of business. Gary took the initiative to lead this operational improvement effort.

CRB had grown both organically in the West Indies and also through acquisition of other smaller local banks such that it now operates in the Caribbean islands of Trinidad, Barbados, St. Vincent, Antigua, St. Lucia, and Jamaica. As a result, CRB maintained a number of different technology platforms, and the policies and practices relating to the processing of personal loans varied somewhat by region. In order to address some of the major technology issues, a new banking system (NBS) had recently been implemented across CRB, providing a common database for all retail banking customers in all geographies and common transactions for deposits, withdrawals, transfers, and foreign-exchange transactions. However, there were challenges in the implementation of NBS, and the many bugs identified its first release presented a huge workload for the IT department.

Gary had a solid case for change and the clear support of the bank's Deputy Managing Director, the General Manager, Retail Banking, and the General Manager, Human Resources. But problems arose when he met with the General Manager (GM) of IT, who flatly stated that his people were stretched to the limit in dealing with the NBS issues, and he did not have the resources to deal with any IT-related requirements that might come out of the Retail Loans Operational Improvement initiative.

Gary raised this issue with the bank's Deputy Managing Director, but made little headway. There were so many demands on the resources of the IT department that Gary needed to accept a major constraint, in that no additional changes would be demanded of the core systems, especially not to NBS.

In spite of this constraint, Gary decided to press ahead, believing that there was ample room for significant improvement even if the IT issues were not addressed. He instructed the working team to focus on those issues that were not IT-related, and to outline the future opportunities for performance improvement once IT resources became available. The project was launched, and the working team made rapid progress. In less than 3 months, the end-to-end loans process in the retail bank was analyzed and designed, and recommendations for implementation developed. At first, Gary and the steering team were pleased with the set of recommendations. There were clear opportunities for reducing client waiting time by refining branch-level policies. The cycle time for loan approval could be reduced by revising CRB's policies on signing authorities in order to empower branch managers to approve loans at higher dollar levels. A number of non-value-added activities were proposed for elimination through streamlining documentation review and audit practices.

However, everyone realized that the truly major gains depended on enhancements to CRB's information systems, involving better online credit reporting, improved imaging capability to replace current manual practices, better funds-transfer technology with direct linkages to the NBS database, and a series of enhancements to the customer relationship management (CRM) system. The GM of Information Systems did not even attend this Steering Team meeting. He remained steadfast in his resolve not to add any further requirements to his already overflowing project list. A full year and a half later, the needed IT refinements for improved performance in processing loans had still not made the top-10 project list in the IT department.

Gary's error was to underestimate the importance of the IT constraint. Just as an army marches on its stomach, a bank lives and dies in accordance with the excellence of its information systems. Leaders need to be cognizant of the potentially debilitating impact of constraints such as "there will be no changes to current information systems," "there will be no changes to current compensation and reward systems," and "there will be no changes to current organization design."

Practically every large improvement effort will rely on IT for optimum success. The IT issues may not be known at the getting-ready stage, but as soon as these do become known, it's essential to fully engage the leaders in IT such that the project becomes their priority, too.

In the analysis and design phases of an improvement project, leaders need to pay close attention to pacing, maintaining momentum, and constructively challenging the designs and plans of the working team. In terms of pacing, any operational improvement project that takes longer than 3 months to go through the stages of getting ready, analysis, and design risks being displaced by other more pressing priorities. The longer it takes to identify and implement improvements, the greater the chance that key people and resources will be diverted to other efforts.[28] In this respect, leaders need to beware of improvement specialists and of the working team taking excessive time to model the current state or measure current operational performance to the seventh significant digit. Operational improvement efforts can be stalled by a failure to focus on pacing, as the following brief example illustrates.

Don, Director for Operational Excellence (OE) at a regional telecommunications company (RTC) was assigned the task of dramatically improving RTC operations through the analysis, design, and implementation of a shared service organization. He worked with the RTC leadership team in defining a vision for shared services and built a solid case for change. Then, he assigned two of his best specialists in the OE department to model and measure the current performance of key processes in RTC. Four months passed, and the walls of the OE war room were plastered with maps and diagrams. Don reviewed the models and found that revision was needed. Some of the models represented a mix of current business practices and desired future business practices, creating confusion.

Once the models had been finally vetted, Don found that the heads of other departments such as HR, Finance, and Procurement were tackling new and more pressing issues. He encountered difficulty in getting the needed resources to launch the shared service improvement effort and eventually the entire effort was placed on the RTC back burner.

The RTC example illustrates the importance of rapidly moving through the getting ready stage. Maintaining momentum and constructively challenging the designs and plans of the working team is yet another area of focus in leading operational improvement. Here, it's essential that executives guide the project team, and failure to do so can have significant adverse consequences, as the following example demonstrates.

Tony, the Vice President of Quality for a U.S. division of a global aerospace company (GAC) had met significant success in improving product quality. Now, he was faced with the challenge of improving GAC's business practices in responding to requests for proposals (RFPs) received from GAC's clients and prospects. The situation was dismal. GAC was failing to respond to RFPs on time around 20% of the time. Clients were not happy, nor were the members of the GAC leadership team. Tony had the full support of both the division's Vice President of Marketing and the Vice President of Engineering and was able to get the needed resources to launch an improvement project. On the surface, the RFP process was fairly standard and easy to understand. When GAC received an RFP, it would be passed to a proposal manager, who would assemble a proposal team comprising the right resources, assess the RFP, and draft a response, which would be approved internally first, and then presented to the client or prospect organization.

Tony launched the project to improve GAC's responsiveness to RFPs. The project team rapidly identified a number of significant issues and opportunities. There was no central point of contact to receive RFPs. Some were received in the Contracts department, others in Marketing, and, at times, an RFP would even be received in Engineering. This sometimes resulted in a delay in passing the RFP to a proposal manager. Due to other priorities, the proposal manager sometimes had difficulty in assembling all the right resources from various other departments. Next, all RFPs were treated more or less in the same way, even though some RFPs were for products that had been quoted in the past 12 months and where the original data was still fresh and current. For the more complex RFPs, and especially for the high-dollar-value ones, there were delays in getting cost estimates. This was particularly relevant when GAC needed to get quotations from its own suppliers on new component parts. Finally, there were frequently delays in getting approval from GAC's own senior management due to the full agendas of GAC leaders and difficulty in getting the needed time to review responses to complex RFPs.

When the project team presented its findings from the analysis phase to the steering team, everyone in the room, including Tony, saw several quick-win opportunities. These included concepts such as establishing an accelerated RFP stream for those RFPs that represented recently quoted products, increasing the threshold for the VP Marketing to approve RFPs on his own, and several other opportunities with short term improvement potential. However, Tony and the other members of the steering team did not step forward and take action on these quick wins. Instead, they congratulated the project team on its work to date and encouraged it to come up with an innovative design that would address all the issues.

It took several weeks for the project team to formalize the recommendations for change to the RFP process. The final set of recommendations did include the quick wins, but these were bundled with other more time-consuming and resource-intensive recommendations. The following main recommendations were tabled: (a) implement an easy-to-monitor (green-yellow-red) measurement system that provided early warning to senior management of responses to RFP that are in jeopardy of missing the due date; (b) build a new database so that cost estimates do not need to be redone every time; (c) create a cost-estimating center of excellence, which would require some organization changes; (d) introduce a super-cross-functional team for larger RFPs; (e) establish a set of tactics designed to get raw-materials information faster and better; and (f) create separate categories for RFPs (normal, super, and fast-track). It is at this point that the second major tactical error in leading operational improvement took place. Instead of providing the project team with constructive feedback and guidance on the sequence of implementing the recommended changes, Tony and the steering team simply assumed that the transition from design to implementation would proceed smoothly. Nothing could have been further from the truth. The project team did make progress in developing the proposed measurement system, but then they got bogged down in defining and creating the cost-estimating center of excellence, as that involved organization change and no small amount of politics. The implementation effort stalled. Tony might had maintained momentum had he encouraged the rapid implementation of the identified quick wins and provided the project team with constructive feedback on the best sequence of implementing the set of recommendations.

As the GAC case illustrates, the challenges in leading operational improvements are all too real. Leaders need to have a better grasp of their roles in formulating a case for change and the tactical aspects of getting ready, pacing, assuring momentum by rapidly capturing quick wins, constructively challenging the designs and plans of the working team, and assuring that the needed elements are in place for implementation success. Part of the problem is that while there is ample guidance on methods and tools, there is little practical guidance available for leaders to develop their skills in leading operational improvement. By way of example, one well-respected firm's executive overview for senior managers of the Define-Measure-Explore-Develop-Implement (DMEDI) method of design for Six Sigma allocated the lion's share of time to the methods and tools in each DMEDI step, and then spent just a few slides during a 2-hour session on the role of leaders in a DMEDI intervention. This also holds for the codified training in other improvement methods. It is somehow assumed that because executives are leaders, they will intuitively know what to do. Nothing is further from the truth. The good news is that there is a better way.

A Better Way

As the existing training for the currently popular methods of operational improvement provides less than adequate guidance on specific leadership practices, there are several things senior managers need to become more adept at doing: learning the fundamentals of change management, establishing context, understanding that each capability has key leverage points, measuring what matters to customers in a disciplined way, forging a strong bond with IT, and learning specific tactics to apply at each stage of an operational improvement project.

The fundamentals of change management have been well documented by John P. Kotter in his seminal book *Leading Change*, and by Kouzes and Posner in their influential work *The Leadership Challenge*. Kotter outlined an eight-step method for leading transformational change in a corporate setting, and Kouzes and Posner detailed 5 practices and 10 commandments of leadership that can be applied in both a corporate environment and our personal lives. Chapter 2 provided an overview of both of these steps and practices, and the original works are effectively required reading for any senior manager wishing to succeed in leading dramatic improvements in operations.[29]

However, the current body of work on leadership does not provide, at least not in sufficient detail, the specific guidance needed for dramatic improvements in operational performance. This is why it's important for senior managers faced with making dramatic improvements in operational performance to establish context and to learn specific tactics to apply at each stage of an operational improvement project.

Thinking in terms of organizational capabilities is arguably the best way of establishing context. An organization's capabilities, or end-to-end processes, if you will, are characterized by the following factors:

- create value for customers;
- drive most discretionary costs;
- can be counted on one hand or, at most, two hands; and
- involve collaboration across two or more corporate functions or departments.[30]

Thinking in terms of organizational capabilities enables organizations to steer the business, understand what is really working and what is not, leverage IT investments, cut costs, improve throughput, and increase agility.

At a high level, the set of capabilities for manufacturing organizations are strikingly similar: introduce new products; market and sell; buy and make; deliver; collect; and provide service. It is the nature of the specific products offered, the culture of the organization, how the organization is structured, and the set of enabling information systems that differentiate how an organization deploys these capabilities. The same can be said for service organizations. The lines of demarcation between manufacturing and service organizations are increasingly blurred. Service organizations in the banking sector, for example, have a set of capabilities that includes introduction of new products or services; marketing and selling these products or services; delivering; collecting; and providing customer service. For service organizations in the utilities sector, such as electric utilities and natural gas providers, the set of capabilities is also similar, with the exception that installation is involved and a network needs to be built and maintained.

There are other important activities that every company engages in, such as hiring, paying, and retaining employees; paying suppliers; producing financial statements; and so on. These activities are not only essential to the business—they can also consume significant costs and are often the focus of many cost-reduction efforts. These support activities do not directly create value for customers, in themselves, but the linkages to core capabilities are often critical. For example, in manufacturing companies that produce on a "make-to-order" basis, the role of procurement in assuring that the right raw materials and components are available on time, complete, and defect-free is instrumental to success. In the service sector, the role of human resources (HR) in attracting, orienting, and retaining staff is instrumental to the success of core capabilities. Yet, in the final analysis, achieving dramatic improvement to operational performance typically revolves around the core, customer-touching capabilities of introducing new products and services, marketing and selling these products and services, delivering or installing these products and services, and responding to customer inquiries and complaints.

Establishing context around key capabilities involves two complementary initiatives: creating a compelling one-page visual schematic of each capability and measuring what matters to both customers and the company. The intent of this one-page schematic is to depict the key capabilities, annotated with the departments that are engaged in delivering each capability, and the related enabling IT systems. Doing so helps the members of the leadership team reach a shared understanding of the definition of core capabilities.

The second activity is a measurement framework that examines operational performance from the two perspectives that were discussed previously and enables measuring what matters to customers in a disciplined way. This framework provides analytical context for key capabilities. Table 4.2 depicts the generic boundaries and metrics for selected capabilities that may be the starting point in creating the right context.

While the capabilities, their boundaries, and even the principal metrics are strikingly similar, the activities inside the boundaries do vary significantly from one company to the next based on how a company is organized, the information systems deployed, and the policies in place. For example, the delivery of product for a manufacturing company that ships from stock involves the key activities of order entry, pick, and pack and ship, while the delivery of new service by an electric utility to a new business customer involves order entry, verification of technical details, ensuring local permits are in place, scheduling installation, and then installing. The way to develop "hard-to-copy" capabilities for competitive advantage resides in the unique combination of linking activities, organization design, measurement, IT enablers, and culture.

Establishing context by way of a one-page schematic that illustrates the boundaries, key activities, the departments involved in key activities,

Table 4.2. Boundaries and Metrics

Capability	Boundaries	Company metrics	Customer metrics
Introduce products	Idea to launch	On budget, Conforms to original specifications	On time (when promised), meets promised functionality
Market/sell	Promote to order	No. of leads, no. of orders, dollar value of orders	Responsive, meets promises
Deliver/install	Order to delivery	No. of orders fulfilled, revenue	On time, complete, no defects
Collect	Invoice to cash	Days of sales outstanding	Accurate, complete, user-friendly
Service	Inquiry to resolution	Cost per call	Resolved correctly the first time

the principal supporting information systems, and the key measures of performance from both company and customer points of view accomplishes several key objectives. It provides a diagram that is useful as a talking tool when communicating the objectives of the case for change of operational improvement efforts. It can stimulate discussion around key leverage points in the selected capability. It can stimulate discussion on the degree of complexity or simplicity of the needed IT systems. Finally, it can serve as a template for people to identify where they contribute to performance. The following brief example illustrates the importance of establishing context and how this promotes thinking at the right level for operational improvement.

> Bill, the Vice President of Operational Excellence (OE) at a diversified chemical company (DCC), believed there were significant opportunities to improve DCC's capability in marketing and selling its products. DCC had a broad product line and three divisions, each of which had its own marketing and sales departments. Bill instructed one of his senior OE specialists to define the market-sell capability across all three divisions and create a one-page schematic that he could use as a talking tool to engage department heads and launch an operational improvement initiative. The resulting document illustrated that the key activities were: promotion of products, receipt of inquiries, engaging with customers, seeking requests for proposals (RFPs), responding to RFPs, and entering orders. Further, it indicated that each division was using a unique sales-contact information management system, that only one of three divisions was capturing customer-oriented measures of performance, and that there was no common RFP database. This schematic was instrumental in assisting Bill as he engaged with the sales and marketing department heads and the Chief Information Officer to determine the scope of the improvements in performance and to identify and gain agreement on key leverage points.

The DCC example illustrates how a high-level schematic of an end-to-end process can be used by leaders to focus their thinking at the right level and avoid diving into too much detail too soon. In order to succeed in dramatically improving operational performance, leaders also need to apply certain key principles and specific tactics at each stage of an operational improvement project. The following are some of the key principles to consider. These principles are supported by a set of characteristics that are outlined in chapter 5.

- *Customer focus.* Establish and sustain an enduring focus on creating value for customers through the measures you monitor, your policies, and your business practices. Become easy to do business with. Recognize the insidious impact of having solely an internal focus. Understand that when you perform for customers, you automatically perform for shareholders.
- *Urgency.* Behave with urgency every day. Never underestimate the power of a good story. Action counts far more than pretty PowerPoint slides. Understand that with urgency and action come some mistakes, and that is OK because that is how most organizations learn and adapt.[31]
- *Right people.* Insist on cross-functional participation and collaboration. Engage the right people from the right departments, especially from IT. Understand that your job is to create a climate that enables people to unleash their full potential. Given the right tools and the right environment, there is no limit to what people can achieve.
- *Role model.* As you are the leader, you need to model the way. Learn by doing. Understand that company policies, recognition, and reward systems must be aligned with desired new behaviors.[32]

The specific tactics that apply to leading operational improvement projects revolve around a series of questions to ask at each stage of a project that relies on the ability to think at the right level. Then, listening carefully and providing feedback is what makes the difference. Table 4.3 outlines some of the typical questions to ask at each of the generic stages of an improvement project.

Thinking at the right level of detail is one of the critical success factors in leading operational improvements. At the definition or scoping stage, it's important to remain at a high level, with a focus on understanding

Table 4.3. Questions That Operational Leaders Might Ask

Stage	Questions to ask
Definition or scoping	• Do we agree on the scope, goals, and schedule? • Do we have the right people? • Is there a tight collaboration with IT? • Is the schedule aggressive yet achievable? • Do we all believe we can win? • Are downstream impacts of any constraints fully understood?
Analysis	• Do we have clarity on the major issues, problems, and opportunities? • To what extent can we quantify the impact of eliminating problems and capitalizing on opportunities? • Do we have the right resources to complete the project on time?
Design	• Is there a solid business case? • Do we have the needed resources for success? • Has IT prioritized this project such that it will be implemented in the planned timeframe?
Implementation	• Do we have a shared commitment to implement the design? • Do we have the needed continuity in terms of resources? • Have we planned for effective communication of changes? • Do we have competent project management? • Have we planned to celebrate success? • Do we have a method in place such that obstacles to implementation can be removed as they occur? • Design principles to be outlined below. • Do we have a shared understanding of current performance from both the customer's and the company's points of view? • Does the design reflect desired principles?* • Do we have a shared understanding of future performance from both the customer's and the company's points of view?

what's required for collaboration and success. At this stage, it's important to avoid diving down into too much detail. That will come later. At the analysis stage, more detail is needed to appreciate the current level of performance, and it's important to refrain from jumping to solutions too early. At the design stage, it is important to develop the ability of asking good probing questions based on a set of design principles that have come to apply universally to operational improvement, even though these were originally introduced in the literature on reengineering.[33] These include the following principles:

- Perform work where it makes the most sense.
- Eliminate non-value-added activities.
- Provide a single point of contact.
- Redesign the process first, and then automate it.
- Ensure 100% quality at the outset.
- Standardize transactional, repetitive activities whenever possible.
- Create innovation in exception handling.
- Capture information once, and at the source.
- Co-locate or use networked teams for complex issues.
- Strive to ensure that the steps in the process are performed in a natural order.
- Reduce checks and controls.
- Minimize reconciliation.
- Take action to enrich jobs by moving from simple tasks to multidimensional work.
- Empower people on the front line.
- Shift the focus of performance measures and compensation shifts from activity to results.
- Change organizational structures from hierarchical to flat.
- Move from multiple databases to one shared database.

Each of these principles can be reframed into a question that can be useful in constructively challenging the recommendations of the project team.

It's at the implementation stage that attention to detail becomes the right level of thinking by senior managers. This stage is also where earlier sins in failing to craft and regularly communicate a compelling case for change, engaging the right people from key departments, measuring performance from the customer's point of view, and assuring the right pacing of improvement activities will become manifest in the form of a decrease in attention and focus. The implementation stage is also where a strong relationship with other departments, such as Human Resources for needed training resources, and IT for the timely roll out of enabling technology, has the greatest impact.

The major pitfalls in the implementation stage of operational improvements to avoid are

- failing to set a high priority on implementing quick wins;
- failing to address obstacles to change promptly as these arise;
- failing to regularly communicate progress and recognize and reward the contributions of project team members;
- lack of attention to assuring that the ingredients to sustain the changes are in place, especially the needed "outside-in" metrics, new work practices enabled through IT, and the formation of a part-time, dedicated team to continuously improve performance;
- lack of continuity of steering team attention and guidance.

Information technology is of particular importance in implementing and sustaining improvements to operational performance. During the earlier stages of operational improvement, the data on what matters to customers in terms of the timely, complete, and error-free delivery of products and services can be assembled rapidly via random sampling. However, this needs to be codified in the implementation stage, and that calls for IT resources. Similarly, the new work methods that may have been role-played and simulated in the earlier stages of operational improvement now have to become routine practice through enabling IT.

The collaboration with IT needs to be forged early on and maintained throughout. In many companies, as the IT department is challenged with maintaining fragmented systems and a long list of project priorities, the early engagement of IT in key operational improvements is an essential, but sometimes difficult to achieve, ingredient. Yet, it is needed to assure that the systems modifications required for planned improvements are high on the IT agenda.

The framework of accountability for operational improvements has to evolve. Given the history of process ownership in reengineering and process management, which is briefly covered in the next chapter, there are some good lessons to be learned.[34] Ideally, the senior executives in charge of various departments would see the need to collaborate and assume joint accountability for the improvement and management of key operational capabilities. But we're not there yet, so some form of interim accountability framework needs to be established. One approach might be to appoint a full-time senior executive with accountability for a major capability. The role of this individual would be to work with the heads of the departments involved in order to radically improve the performance of the capability in question and then assure that the infrastructure for continuous improvement is in place. For example, the executive for the new product development capability would need to work with Research and Development, Marketing, Sales, Production, Customer Service , and IT to assure that new products are introduced faster and better and yield greater results. The alignment of compensation systems for senior executives is absolutely needed here. This is one of the areas where we have the most to learn—establishing a framework of accountability for operational improvements.

Chapter Summary

The historical odds of success in successfully leading major change efforts has hovered around 30%, and this has had little to do with a deficit in improvement methods, tools, or even management advice. Most of today's popular improvement methods evolved from the work of W. Edwards Deming, Joseph M. Juran, and the quality movement of the 1970s and 1980s.

The proliferation of improvement methods over the past two decades has led many companies to deploy two or more methods in an attempt to wring improved performance from operations, which often leads to multiple, disconnected efforts, with each group advocating that their approach is *the* best way, leading to a competition for resources. A comparison of the obstacles to success with Six Sigma and Lean (presented in Table 4.1) indicates some common themes.

The role of senior managers is to provide guidance and feedback at each stage of an improvement project: getting ready, taking action, and sustaining change. Leaders need to have a better grasp of their roles in formulating a case for change, and the tactical aspects of getting ready, pacing, assuring momentum by rapidly capturing quick wins, constructively challenging the designs and plans of the working team, and assuring that the needed elements are in place for implementation success.

The failure to appreciate the downstream impact of constraints and failure to guide the project team is illustrated by way of examples. The ability to ask good, probing questions is an important skill set for operational leaders. Table 4.3 depicts some of the questions that operational leaders may ask at key points in an improvement project. At a high level, while the capabilities, their boundaries, and even the principal metrics may appear strikingly similar, the activities inside the boundaries do vary significantly from one company to the next based on how a company is organized, the information systems deployed, and the policies in place.

The successful implementation of operational improvements is rarely limited to just workflow considerations and often involves other factors, such as job designs, information system issues, structural changes, new measures, revised business rules, skills training, and the like. The development of new and improved measurement and management practices is needed in order to sustain performance improvement.

The way to develop "hard to copy" capabilities for competitive advantage resides in the unique combination of linking activities, organization design, measurement, IT enablers, and culture. The framework of accountability for operational improvements has to further evolve in the future. Ideally, the senior executives in charge of various departments would see the need to collaborate and assume joint accountability for the improvement and management of key operational capabilities. But since we're not there yet, some interim mechanism appears to be needed.

CHAPTER 5

Sustaining Improvements

According to a survey of 769 global CEOs, excellence of execution is the top-ranked concern for CEOs worldwide.[1] This finding reflects that only about 30 to 40% of reengineering and Six Sigma projects achieve their stated objectives and also a deep concern with sustaining gains from operational improvements.

Operational improvement projects, by definition, have a clear beginning and an end. When it comes to sustaining these gains, the emphasis needs to evolve to governance and continuous improvement from project management. Here, we appear to have less clarity on the historical level of sustainable performance, but the general sense is that organizations' track record in sustaining the gains from improvement efforts is not particularly good. Executives regularly express frustration with the challenges in sustaining the gains from change programs. Also, process improvement professionals periodically remark on the need to improve or redesign the same process that was addressed just a few years ago. The relative lack of success in sustaining process change may be part of the reason why organizations drift from one method of process improvement to another over time.

While most firms are becoming increasingly adept at executing improvements to their operations in projects of small scope, many firms continue to struggle when it comes to executing projects of larger scope that require broad cross-functional collaboration. And this is amplified when it comes to sustaining the changes from dramatic improvements to operational performance.

Change can only be sustained when new behaviors "become the way we do things around here."[2] In order to institutionalize change, an ongoing program of communication is needed to assist people in the organization in appreciating how the new ways of working have actually had a positive impact on performance. This implies a need for sustaining a measurement system that continuously monitors performance from both the company's and the customer's points of view, for, as the old dictum states, "it's what organizations measure that they manage." Other major elements of sustaining change, especially when it comes to sustaining the improvement of organizational capabilities, include the means to make common goals, ongoing cross-functional commitment, continuous improvement, and periodic celebration an essential part of the organization's fabric.

Challenges in Sustaining Improvements

In order to sustain improvements in operational performance, it's essential that the new performance measures become part of the scorecard that leaders periodically review and that the organization expend energy in continuous improvement. The appointment of a new CEO, wholesale changes in organization structure, and shifting priorities are just a few of the events that can disrupt the sustainment of major change.

The appointment of a new CEO can impede the sustainment of operational improvements, especially when the new CEO is determined to put his or her stamp on the organization. In such a case, anything that was done by the previous CEO may become objectionable, as was the case in the following example.

> John, the Chief Financial Officer at a regional division of a large oil and gas company (OGC), was pleased with the progress that OGC had made on a number of operational fronts. OGC had identified key capabilities in terms of acquisition, exploration and development, production, and marketing and sales. John had also implemented improvement projects in each area over the past couple of years. The gains from these projects were impressive, in part due to improved collaboration among the key department heads. The visible support for these efforts by OGC's CEO, a new scoreboard used at OGC's monthly operating reviews, and an ongoing program of communications on successes and challenges contributed to sustaining, and even extending, these gains.
>
> Then, OGC's CEO retired. The newly appointed CEO did not see things the same way. He was quick to bring in a team

of top consultants to reformulate strategy. Then he made several changes to key senior managers involved in the exploration and development and the sales and marketing areas. Also, he spent little time on the new performance metrics at operational review meetings and renewed the focus on the traditional financial metrics of performance. John could see a gradual decline in the level of collaboration as a new leadership team evolved. The gains in operational improvement began to erode. While John had a cordial business relationship with the new CEO, there was little he could do on his own, and John was only a couple of years away from retirement himself. The visible erosion to OGC's operational performance took less than a year.

The appointment of a new CEO who simply sees things differently represents perhaps the most menacing threat to sustaining operational improvement; however, a sudden shift in priorities or a massive change in organization structure are equally dangerous. When there is a wholesale change to organization structure, even without a change in the leader at the top, the focus of middle managers understandably shifts from improving operations to establishing relationships with a new boss and new peers. Similarly, a sudden shift in priorities can serve to derail previous efforts to improve operational performance. Most notably, when a company faces financial challenges, it is common to see the traditional financial measures of performance, and a focus on "actual to budget," displace prior efforts to improve customer satisfaction. While there is no panacea or magic potion for sustainability, companies can mitigate these threats to sustaining improvements in operational performance by engaging in the management practices outlined in this chapter.

Tactics for Sustainability

It is difficult enough to achieve the levels of collaboration and discipline needed to dramatically improve a core capability. Sustaining, and even enhancing, the improvements over time arguably represents an even greater challenge. Much can be learned from the literature on process management, where it has been argued that success in process improvement and management is a "team sport."[3] The following management practices can optimize sustainability of improvements in operational performance such that the new behaviors become "the way we do things around here":

- Continue to monitor the metrics that matter to both customers and the company.
- Assign explicit accountability for ongoing operational performance.
- Maintain an infrastructure for continuous improvement, stressing cross-departmental collaboration and aligning recognition and reward systems supported with an ongoing program of communication.

The combination of these management practices can institutionalize a new way of working. However, note that all of these practices need to be put into practice in order to achieve the degree of collaboration, discipline, and focus that is needed to mitigate threats to sustainability.

Measuring what matters to customers is one of the fundamental cornerstones of the structure needed for sustainability. The factors that customers care about, such as perfect orders and responsiveness, can drive ongoing cross-departmental cooperation. Consider the following examples:

- In a manufacturing company, measuring the percentage of orders delivered on time, complete, and defect-free can encourage Sales, Manufacturing, Production, IT, and Operations to work together to achieve desired results.
- In a bank, measuring the percentage of loans provided on time (at least when promised, preferably when requested) and accurately can encourage Origination, Operations, Underwriting, and IT to work together to achieve desired results.
- In a company involved with the installation of new service, such as cable TV or landline phone companies, measuring the percentage of orders installed on time, complete, and defect-free can encourage Sales, Customer service, Network Operations, IT, and Field Operations to work together to achieve desired results.

- In a health insurance company, measuring the percentage of first-time right responses to health care providers' inquiries and complaints can encourage the Medical Policy, Customer Service, and Claims to work together to achieve desired results.

Note that measuring the traditional financial metrics of performance, such as volume and revenue, does not do much to promote cross-departmental collaboration, as each department will naturally focus primarily only on its own role. What typically results is a certain amount of finger-pointing.

By measuring what matters to customers, a company's senior managers will be more inclined to ask the relevant types of questions that drill into the root causes of failing to meet desired results for customers. For example, at a typical business-to-business manufacturing firm that makes custom products, activities in the "order to delivery" capability typically comprise several activity sets or subprocesses, including order entry, procuring components, production, order packing, and order shipping. The end-to-end activity, or process perspective, allows a firm to identify the elements of accuracy, cost, timeliness, and productivity for each of these activity sets or processes as they combine to produce the final output, which creates value for both the customer and the company. When the percentage of orders delivered on time, complete, and defect-free is below the desired level, department heads can ask meaningful questions around the root causes in areas such as lack of order accuracy, delays or errors in procuring needed components, delays or errors in production scheduling and production, or delays in expediting. Best results are obtained when the senior leadership team regularly reviews and discusses performance from the customer's point of view, when there is a structure that assigns accountability for such performance, when middle-manager and employee recognition and reward systems are aligned with desired performance for customers, and when an infrastructure for continuous improvement is in place that encourages collaboration across departments.

Assigning explicit accountability for operational performance is the second of these four management practices that, in combination, can serve to sustain improvements. In this respect, the lessons learned in

examining the role of a process owner in both reengineering and process management can provide useful insights. An organizational capability, much like an end-to-end process, requires that different departments
work together. In traditional organizations, there is generally no one
individual who has overall accountability for these large sets of value-
creating activities. The concept of a process owner has been proposed
in both the process management and reengineering literature as the best
means of assigning accountability for process performance.[4] The role of
the process owner has been described as one that is focused on the effective improvement and management of an end-to-end business process.
Process owners have been described as senior managers, with credibility
and clout, who drive collaboration across departments and motivate and
advise both project teams and continuous-improvement teams.[5] There
are two common models for process ownership. In one model, key executives wear two hats, one for their business or functional responsibility
and another for monitoring, improving, and managing the performance
of an enterprise-level business process. In the other model, a senior staff
person is appointed as dedicated process owner, with the responsibility to
work with department heads to improve and manage core processes. The
experience of companies as diverse as Air Products and Chemicals, Caterpillar, Duke Power, IBM, Owens Corning, Nokia, and Texas Instruments
in establishing some form of process ownership has been documented.[6]

In spite of the extensive literature, and no small amount of fanfare
around process owners, one is hard pressed to find success stories of
the beneficial and enduring impact of process ownership on organizational performance. Organizations often stumble in sustaining meaningful and ongoing success with process ownership in some or all of
the following ways:

- Process owners are appointed at middle management levels
  with responsibility for processes of small scope and are not
  supported by executive process-owner appointments for
  the improvement and management of the firm's end-to-end
  processes.
- There is a lack of adequate and continuing training and educa-
  tion on the role of the process owner.

- The role of the process owner is divorced from the fundamental management framework of the firm and process owners lack a clear voice in making decisions around resources and priorities.

The relative lack of success with process ownership may be due to one or more of the following factors. First, the increasing complexity of organization structures, where there are often already matrix-reporting relationship, by either geographic or product lines, and where people simply do not have the capacity to overlay yet another level of complexity, makes it increasingly difficult to install and sustain process ownership. Second, the lack of longevity of process owners may be due to an ongoing obsession by senior leaders on tinkering with organization design, combined with the advice of some thought leaders to "get the right people on the bus," which results in a never-ending series of reorganizations and restructurings. Finally, it may simply be due to the perception that a process perspective threatens the traditional functional view of organizations, and as this latter view has been entrenched in corporate cultures for over a century, the functional perspective prevails.

The insights from the experience of process ownership in reengineering and process management would appear to indicate that organizations that accept the importance of assigning explicit accountability for operational performance should

- minimize the threat to functional thinkers or accept that the senior people who persist in thinking in this way will need to be replaced;
- endeavor not to create yet another level of complexity in organizational structure;
- ensure that there are real consequences, both positive and negative, in fulfilling this role and that it represents a distinct career advancement opportunity for fast-track middle management;[7]
- install a strong alignment of reward systems by allocating a significant portion of the discretionary component of bonus compensation to achieving specific improvements in operational performance.

This would argue in favor of appointing one, or at most a few, senior managers in change-agent positions who would work with all of the department heads in a collaborative way to improve and manage operational performance. The intent of this role would be to assist the organization in making the transition to a model where heads of departments assume shared accountability for operational performance. Ideally, in a manufacturing company, the heads of R&D and Marketing and Production would jointly share accountability for new product introduction, and the department heads in Customer Service and Operations would jointly share accountability for order fulfillment and the like. In a network-based service organization, the heads of Engineering and Network Operations and Marketing would jointly share accountability for new service introduction, and the department heads in Customer Service and Field Operations would jointly share accountability for new service installation and the like.

Assigning accountability for operational performance cannot succeed in sustaining the gains from improvement projects unless there is some infrastructure installed for continuous improvement and recognition, and reward systems are aligned with desired results at multiple levels in the organization. The principal ingredients for this infrastructure are:

- an agreed-upon set of performance metrics to be used in monitoring operational performance, which is reviewed by the senior leadership team regularly;
- a senior manager who is accountable and is compensated in accordance with achieving defined results, for dramatic improvements in the operational performance of a key capability and for its continuous improvement;
- a standing, part-time, cross-functional project team that acts to continuously improve performance;
- a standing, part-time steering team, which accepts the responsibility of overcoming obstacles to continuous improvement as identified by the project team;
- visible and meaningful incentives to work cross-functionally at senior and middle management levels;
- an ongoing communication program that engages employees in continuous improvement.

An ongoing communication program that engages employees in continuous improvement is instrumental to long-term success. This is where companies often stumble. Leaders often have the view that once an improvement project has been assessed to yield desired results, it is then time to move on to the next challenge. But this is not so. By maintaining an ongoing communication program that emphasizes the need to continuously improve, supported with visible measures of performance and aligned rewards and recognition systems, employees will find ways to further improvements.

There are also certain leadership characteristics that are central to the success of change agents and senior managers who wish to succeed in leading dramatic improvements in operational performance. People are born with some of the essential characteristics, and others can be learned. Honesty, truthfulness, integrity, and sincerity are characteristics people are born with. But other traits, such as discipline, realism, and thoroughness can be learned. Success in operational leadership has much to do with the following traits or characteristics: disciplined, inspirational, realistic, enthusiastic, collaborative, and thorough (DIRECT).

Leaders who are DIRECT are disciplined. They set clear goals and priorities and monitor progress toward these. They are able to think at the right level and can frame the issues around organizational capabilities in simple, visually compelling diagrams. They think and act both systemically and systematically. They believe in the dictum "In God we trust—all others must present evidence." DIRECT leaders have the ability to inspire. They understand the power of good story and search for ways to directly involve employees. They understand the importance of framing stories in such a way that each story has both a positive (imagine the possibilities) and a negative theme (what is the problem?). They listen well. They empathize with people and care deeply about the work that people do. They recognize that the factors that are important to senior management—such as competitive position, reducing costs, and increasing net profit—are often less important to employees. Instead, inspirational leaders sense that employees are motivated by stories involving factors such as improving customer service, making a contribution to some greater social good, improving their own working environment, and realizing the potential for personal rewards through either bonus compensation or visible recognition. DIRECT leaders are realistic. They are candid regarding the current level of performance and are able to measure it from the perspective of the company and the customer. They do not shy away from embarrassing statistics. For example, a realistic leader will not be satisfied in measuring on-time performance in terms of the variance in the date promised by the company. They will also measure it in accordance with the variance to the date requested by the customer, even if that metric has not historically been used by the organization to assess current performance. Also, they understand that technology is available to all, but how it is applied is what counts. DIRECT leaders are also enthusiastic. They act with urgency and passion. They are curious and love to ask "what if" questions. DIRECT leaders are collaborative. They understand that no one department creates value for customers on its own, and collaboration across departments, and sometimes across company boundaries, is essential in today's business environment. They appreciate that to earn trust, you first have to give it. Finally, DIRECT leaders are thorough. They know the business from both a workflow and an organization design perspective. They value the increasing importance of information systems. They follow up. They understand that even small rewards have a disproportionately positive impact on employees to motivate engagement in change that can last for months.[8]

When organizations appoint senior managers who possess the DIRECT characteristics and behaviors as change agents to improve operational performance, they can influence leadership behavior such that the organization engages in a continuing cycle of defining, improving, monitoring, and evaluating its core capabilities. Once these management practices become integrated into the fabric of the organization, it will achieve greater agility and be able to "turn on a dime."

Chapter Summary

Excellence of execution has become the top-ranked concern for CEOs. This has as much to do with sustaining gains as with raising the bar on the success rate of improvement projects.

Change can best be sustained when the set of new behaviors "become the way we do things around here." In order to institutionalize change, an ongoing program of communication, a measurement system that continuously monitors performance from both the company's and the customer's points of view, common goals, ongoing cross-functional commitment, continuous improvement, and periodic celebration are needed. The appointment of a new CEO, wholesale changes in organization structure, and shifting priorities are arguably the key events that disrupt the sustainment of major change.

Appropriate management practices relating to metrics, accountability, and an infrastructure for continuous improvement can optimize sustainability of improvements in operational performance such that the new behaviors become institutionalized.

Key lessons learned from the experience of process owners in reengineering and process management were reviewed. The main areas where organizations appear to stumble in process ownership were summarized. The principal elements of creating an infrastructure for continuous improvement were listed. In light of the less than stellar experience with process ownership, it was proposed that a few senior managers appointed in change-agent positions, who would work with all the department heads in a collaborative way to improve and manage operational performance, may be a better way.

Success in operational leadership has much to do with the traits implicit in the DIRECT model, representing the characteristics of discipline, inspiration, realism, enthusiasm, collaboration, and thoroughness. When operational leadership is practiced in a DIRECT way, a new mode of operations may well lead to achieving greater agility.

CHAPTER 6

The Future

What will be the role of operational leadership in the future as organizations continue their search for competitive advantage? That's what this final chapter explores.

If you aspire to improve the level of operational leadership in your organization, you will progress in the following areas:

- making sense of the glut of management advice from thought leaders and gurus;
- coming to terms with the linkage of strategy and execution;
- organizing various improvement methods under an umbrella program;
- crafting a close, collaborative relationship with the leaders in IT; and
- developing a set of the appropriate leadership mindset and behaviors needed for success.

Management Advice

There is a lot of very good management advice out there. In fact, there's an overabundance of management advice, and often, management gurus dive deep into their practice area without exploring all of the relevant linkages to related domains. Instead of searching for just the right guru, leaders will begin to look for common themes. They are likely to find them without searching too hard, for the fact is that management advice evolves at a slow pace, with each thought leader taking the previous body of work just one small step further and adding his or her special spin on what was already known. Just consider the contents of Table 6.1, which represents excerpts from highly regarded management advice. Do you see any common themes?

Table 6.1. Management Advice

What really works[1]	The knowing-doing gap[2]	Execution[3]	The agenda[4]
Devise a clearly stated, focused strategy.	Put why before how.	Execution is a discipline.	Make your company easy to do business with.
Develop flawless operational execution.	Knowing comes from doing.	Execution is the major job of the business leader.	Focus on the final customer.
Create a performance-oriented culture.	Action counts more than elegant plans.	Execution must be a core element of a company's culture.	Use measurement for improving, not accounting.
Build a fast, flexible, flat company structure.	Measure what matters.	Make it clear that rewards and respect are based on performance.	Add more value for your customers.
Hold on to people who show talent and find more of them.	There is no doing without mistakes.		Loosen up your organizational structure.
Keep leadership committed to the business.	What leaders do matters.		Knock down walls by collaborating wherever you can.

Strategy and Execution

Both strategy and execution matter enormously. Thoughtful leaders will recognize that there are only a handful of strategic options. What matters are the set of customers you elect to serve, the markets you elect to pursue, and the products you choose to offer. It also matters what you choose *not* to do.[5] Understand that strategy cannot be effectively executed solely by individual departments. Flawless execution calls for collaboration across departments, and these days, even across companies. Dramatic improvement of core capabilities is central to execution. The critical few capabilities, which require cross-functional collaboration, represent the essence of a hard-to-copy execution of strategy as they embody the entirety of workflow, information technology, decision rights, and customer focus.

Competing on capabilities requires an enduring focus on customers. A customer-centric view of the business enables the development of a clearly stated, focused strategy in two ways. First, measuring a company's current performance in satisfying customer requirements with respect to metrics—such as quality, timeliness, completeness, and responsiveness—will allow a company to more realistically assess where it stands in terms of providing customers with what they expect and deserve. Then, a core capability perspective enables the firm to articulate which of its capabilities needs to be improved, and by how much, in order to deliver on its strategy. Thinking in terms of organizational capabilities enables organizations to steer the business, understand what's really working and what is not, leverage IT investments, cut costs, improve throughput, and increase agility. In so doing, you will come to appreciate that it's possible to achieve a more lucid roadmap for key strategic initiatives, and your company will set the stage to confront the brutal facts in terms of the size of performance gaps to be bridged.

Organizing Operational Improvements

There are a lot of useful improvement methods, but most are just a set of tools. What's needed is an umbrella program that focuses on performing for customers. It doesn't much matter what this is called. Some companies call it "operational excellence," others call it "operational effectiveness," and there are other good names, too. But what is important is that the various improvement methods in use within the company be organized under an umbrella and that tools be selected for deployment based on the scope and nature of the needed improvement in operational performance. This also means that companies dedicated to improving operational performance should designate a senior manager, reporting directly to the CEO, to lead operational improvements and work closely with the heads of departments to develop greater and lasting cross-functional collaboration. The success factors are well known. Simply consider the following points of advice, adapted from the experience of Dr. Joseph Juran:[6]

- The chief executive personally leads the initiative.
- The company trains the entire managerial hierarchy in operational improvement.

- The company ensures the business plan includes operational improvement goals.
- The goals emphasize improving at a revolutionary rate, year after year.
- The company sets up the means to measure progress against goals.
- The senior managers review progress regularly.
- The company provides for participation by the work force.
- The company develops a system of recognition for superior performance.
- Annual improvement is one of the essential success factors; without it there can be no operational leadership.
- It is a big advantage for companies to have available a field-tested, proven managerial process as an aid to operational improvement.
- Training is needed to enable company personnel to attain mastery of the operational improvements.
- The training should include participating in actual improvement projects.

Ask yourself, how many of the above apply within your organization? Then, ask yourself who is accountable for improvements to operational performance? It cannot *just* be the Chief Operating Officer (COO), although that is certainly a key role. In the future, organizations will come to recognize that senior executives need to be appointed key change agents, aligned with the company's core capabilities to fundamentally improve how businesses get products or services developed, sold, delivered, and serviced. That's because the century-old focus on functional departments is not likely to evolve without some effort. Note that this is in stark contrast to current practices with improvement methods such as Lean and Six Sigma, which rely, in one way or another, on a champion for a project that has a beginning and an end. It differs from the concept of a reengineering czar. The concept of appointing senior change agents on a continuing basis for each major capability is more in line with the practice of process ownership from the domain of process management and BPM, but with one important difference. The role of this individual is to work with the department heads involved in a specific capability, in order to radically improve the performance of the capability in question, and then assure that the infrastructure for continuous improvement is in place. For example, the executive accountable for the new product development capability would work with the department heads in R&D, Marketing, Sales, Production, Customer Service, and IT to assure that new products are introduced faster and better and yield greater results. The executive accountable for the customer acquisition capability would work with the department heads in Marketing, Sales, Production, Customer Service, and IT to assure that customer acquisition and retention perform optimally on a sustainable basis. Only by investing in a senior resource for each major capability will companies be able to assure continuing management attention on cross-functional collaboration and the sustained visibility of customer-focused metrics on the scoreboard of the senior leadership team.

Your Best Friend

A close relationship with IT is essential in order to achieve dramatic improvement in operational performance. Practically every organization capability relies on IT, and enhancements to information systems are critical in taking improvement action and sustaining change. As the IT profession is still relatively young when compared to other functional disciplines such as sales, production, and finance, the challenge of bridging the infamous IT-business divide remains. You, as an operational leader, can help the CIO in this respect. And you will need the CIO's assistance, as practically any large improvement project will be faced with relational databases that do not relate, help desks that do not help, and tracking systems that do not track what is needed. You will therefore benefit from a close collaboration with IT that is established early in the life cycle of projects and builds as projects go through key stages.

Recognize that IT has its own challenges. Over the years, IT departments have had to cope with the disruptive impact of integrating incompatible IT systems resulting from mergers and acquisitions and fulfilling requests by different departments. Along the way, many companies have created or purchased dozens of legacy information systems, each consisting of countless lines of code that do not "talk" to one another. As the data needed by various departments is collected in separate databases, more interfaces are needed, and these are hard to maintain and require more IT resources simply to keep up with day-to-day tasks.

If you have a long-term view on operational performance, the CIO may become your best friend. By working together you can address several fundamental issues that require close IT-business collaboration, such as how much should we spend on IT systems and applications, which core capabilities are most in need of IT investments, what risks should we jointly accept, and who should take the credit for successful projects and the blame for failures?[7]

Framing performance in the context of core capabilities facilitates a more meaningful discussion of the return that can be expected from investments in IT, which in turn leads to more informed decisions regarding which capabilities are most in need of investment in IT. A close collaboration with IT can create more clarity on the size of the prize and the risks of failure, and can lead to joint accountability for IT-enabled projects to improve operational performance.

There's a good chance that the needed IT-operational leadership can be developed. Both professions share many of the same challenges listed below:

- lack of high-level, visible measures;
- challenges in engaging executive sponsors;
- lack of investment in training;
- too many projects;
- too many hard-to-control interdependencies; and
- hard-to-maintain executive attention.

The partnership with IT can also lead to other benefits for the organization. Focusing on core capabilities as the means for executing strategy can facilitate a closer link of IT plans with strategic direction. Viewing the business from the outside-in as well as the inside-out can give IT a different perspective on performance and may form the basis of a transition to a more integrated technology platform. Working together to dramatically improve operational performance can assist IT in becoming recognized as having a better understanding of the business and contribute to a greater performance orientation. Emphasizing the improvement of core capabilities or large end-to-end workflows can assist IT in developing a more unified technology platform.[8] The use of evolving IT tools and methods such as business process management systems (BPMS) and services oriented architectures (SOA) can be deployed to fundamentally change the way work is done and embed new work practices for sustainability. This is something that's essential to an operational leader.

The Right Mindset

What else is needed for organizations to achieve competitive advantage? A shift in conventional wisdom and different leadership mindset and behavior. This is a journey that invariably calls for a customer-focused and performance-oriented CEO and senior management team. What that involves is depicted in Table 6.2. How important is this? Note that over 50% of how employees perceive their organization's climate can be traced to the actions of leaders.[9]

Table 6.2. *Leadership Mindset and Behavior*

Leadership mindset	Leadership behavior
• Think systemically and systematically. • View the business from the customer's perspective. • Imagine. Collaborate. • Trust middle-management teams—they are closer to the way work is done. • Believe in the value of measuring and rewarding performing for customers. • Understand that technology is available to all—it is how you apply it that counts. • Appreciate that what gets measured gets done and what gets rewarded gets done consistently. • Know that language, technology, and decision rights are some of the primary determinants of culture.	• Develop an enduring view on performing for customers. • Collaborate on the design of core capabilities to deliver on business goals. • Assure that organization design, as defined by structure, measures, and rewards, enables the organization to perform for customers. • Deploy enabling information technology to enable operational performance. • Tightly link a customer-centric performance measurement system to budgets and operational reviews. • Deploy a set of integrated methods and tools to embed new work practices.

A large part of developing the right mindset revolves around an enduring focus on what matters to customers and the intelligent and disciplined use of analytics.[10] A more disciplined focus on measuring what matters to customers may not in itself guarantee better results, but it can lead to better decisions.

This is a tall order. Make sense of the glut of management advice from thought leaders and gurus. Come to terms with the linkage of strategy and execution. Organize various improvement methods under an umbrella program. Craft a close, collaborative relationship with the leaders in information systems, especially the CIO. Develop a set of the appropriate leadership mindset and behaviors needed for success. If it were easy, everyone would be doing it. But it is far from easy, and that is why the companies who succeed in these areas in the future will be able to better guide the business, meet customer needs, leverage IT investments, cut costs, improve throughput, and increase agility, or, in a phrase, attain competitive advantage through operational leadership.

Notes

Chapter 1

1. Stalk (2008).
2. Shapiro, Rangan, and Sviolka (1992).
3. Hammer (2001a).
4. Kotter (1995).
5. See the July 2008 issue of *McKinsey Quarterly* for a survey on organizational transformation.
6. Chakravorty (2010).
7. Hammer (2004, April).
8. Davenport (1993).
9. Davenport and Beck (2000).
10. This view has been proposed by a number of authors, including Andrew Spanyi in *More for less* and Barbara Bund in *The outside-in corporation*.
11. Porter (1996).
12. Davenport (1993); Rummler and Brache (1995).
13. Drucker (1999).
14. Krames (2008).
15. Davenport (1993); Rummler and Brache (1995).
16. Ross and Weill (2002).
17. Davenport, Harris, and Morison (2010).
18. Herrington, Malone, and Georges (2008).

Chapter 2

1. Kotter (1996).
2. Banerji, Leinwand, and Mainardi (2009).
3. Kehoe (2002) suggested that up to 50% of CRM implementations fail to achieve stated objectives, and as many as one in five may actually damage customer relationships.
4. Hammer (2001b).
5. Bartholomew (2004).
6. http://www.gartner.com/it/page.jsp?id=497088.
7. Several of these points are also addressed in John Kotter's (1995) article "Leading change: Why transformation efforts fail."

Chapter 3

1. Porter (1980).
2. Porter (1980).
3. Treacy and Wiersema (1995).
4. Porter (1996).
5. A more full treatment of these attributes can be found in Treacy and Wiersema (1995).
6. Galbraith (2005).
7. Brache (2002).

Chapter 4

1. Hammer (1990).
2. The Rapid Results Method is offered by Robert H. Schaffer and Associates and is outlined in the book *Rapid results: How 100-day projects build the capacity for large scale change* (Jossey-Bass, 2005). The Accelerating Corporate Transformation (ACT) method was outlined by Robert H. Miles in his January 2010 article in *Harvard Business Review*.
3. Hammer (2002).
4. Spanyi (2006).
5. Hammer and Goding (2001).
6. Spanyi (2006).
7. Emiliani and Stec (2005).
8. Emiliani and Stec (2005).
9. Swank (2003).
10. Cooper and Maskell (2008).
11. Hammer (1990).
12. Hammer and Champy (2001).
13. Hammer (2001b).
14. Davenport (1993).
15. Rummler and Brache (1995).
16. Spanyi (2006); Hammer (2002).
17. Spanyi (2003).
18. Chakravorty (2010).
19. Emiliani and Stec (2005).
20. Spanyi (2006).
21. Emiliani and Stec (2005).
22. Miles (2010).
23. Ashkenas (2009).
24. Beer and Nohria (2000).
25. Cooper (1993).

26. The stage-gate concept was introduced by Dr. Robert Cooper (1993), and has since been developed extensively. For details, see http://*www.stage-gate.com*.

27. Ballé and Ballé (2009).

28. Chakravorty (2010).

29. Kotter's book *A sense of urgency* (2008) provides more details on this important aspect of leading change.

30. Banerji, Leinwand, and Mainardi (2009).

31. Kotter (2008).

32. Pfeffer and Sutton (2000).

33. Hammer (2001a).

34. The topic of process ownership has been promoted for two decades, initially, by Rummler and Brache (1990), then by Hammer and Champy (1993), Hammer (2001a), Spanyi (2006), and several others. However, the sustainability of process ownership remains problematic.

Chapter 5

1. See the Conference Board report, *CEO challenge 2007: Top 10 challenges*.

2. Kotter (1995).

3. Spanyi (2003).

4. This point has been made by several authors, including, but not limited to, Rummler and Brache (1995) and Hammer (2001a).

5. Hammer (2001a).

6. Spanyi (2006).

7. Ramias and Wilkins (2009).

8. Aiken and Keller (2009).

Chapter 6

1. Joyce, Nohria, and Robertson (2003).

2. Pfeffer and Sutton (2000).

3. Bossidy and Charan (2002).

4. Hammer (2001a).

5. Brache (2002).

6. Juran (2002).

7. Ross and Weill (2002).

8. Feld and Stoddard (2004).

9. Goleman, Boyatzis, and McKee (2002).

10. Davenport, Harris, and Morison (2010).

References

Aiken, C., & Keller, S. (2009). The irrational side of change. *McKinsey Quarterly, 2.*

Ashkenas, R. (2009). Yes, you can simplify your organization. Retrieved August 17, 2009 from http://www.forbes.com.

Ballé, M., & Ballé, F. (2009). *The lean manager: A novel of lean transformation.* Cambridge, MA: Lean Enterprise Institute.

Banerji, S., Leinwand, P., and Mainardi, C. R. (2009). *Cut costs and grow stronger: A strategic approach to what to cut and what to keep.* Harvard Business School Press.

Bartholomew, D. (2004). The ABCs of ERP. *CFO Magazine.* Retrieved October 5, 2004 from http://www.cfo.com.

Barwise, P., & Meehan, S. (2004). *Simply better: Winning and keeping customers by delivering what matters most.* Harvard Business School Press.

Beer, M., and Nohria, N. (2000). Cracking the code of change. *Harvard Business Review (78)*3: 133–141.

Bossidy, L., & Charan, R. (2002). *Execution: The discipline of getting things done.* Crown Business.

Brache, A. (2001). *How organizations work.* Wiley.

Bund, B. (2005). *The outside-in corporation: How to build a customer-centric organization for breakthrough results.* McGraw-Hill.

Chakravorty, S. (2010, January 25). Where process-improvement projects go wrong. *The Wall Street Journal.*

Cooper, R., & Maskell, B. (2008). How to manage through worse-before-better. *Sloan Management Review (49)*4: 58–65.

Cooper, R. G. (1993). *Winning at new products: Accelerating the process from idea to launch.* Perseus Books.

Davenport, T. H. (1993). *Process innovation.* Harvard Business School Press.

Davenport, T. H. (1998). Putting the enterprise into the enterprise system. *Harvard Business Review (76)*41: 121–131.

Davenport, T. H., & Beck, J. C. (2000). Getting the attention you need. *Harvard Business Review (78)*5: 118–126.

Davenport, T. H., Harris, J. G., & Morison, R. (2010). *Analytics at work: Smarter decisions, better results.* Harvard Business School Press.

Drucker, P. (1999) *Management challenges of the 21st century.* Harper Business.

Emiliani, M.L., & Stec, D.J. (2005). Leaders Lost in Transformation, *Leadership & Organization Development Journal (26)*5.

Feld, C. S., & Stoddard, D. B. (2004). Getting IT right. *Harvard Business Review (82)*2: 72–79.

Galbraith, J. R. (2005). *Designing the customer-centric organization: A guide to strategy, structure and process.* Jossey-Bass.

Goleman, D., Boyatzis, R., & McKee, A. (2002). *Primal leadership: Realizing the power of emotional intelligence.* Harvard Business School Press.

Hammer, M. (1990). Reengineering work: Don't automate, obliterate. *Harvard Business Review (68)*4: 104–112.

Hammer, M. (2001a). *The agenda.* Crown Business.

Hammer, M. (2001b). The superefficient company. *Harvard Business Review (79)*8: 82–91.

Hammer, M. (2002). Process management and the future of Six Sigma. *Sloan Management Review (43)*2: 26–32.

Hammer, M. (2004). Deep change. *Harvard Business Review (82)*4: 84–93.

Hammer, M., & Champy, J. (2001). *Reengineering the corporation: A manifesto for business revolution.* Harper Business.

Hammer, M., & Goding, J. (2001). Putting Six Sigma in perspective. *Quality (40)*10: 58–63.

Hammer, M., & Stanton, S. (1999). How process enterprises really work. *Harvard Business Review (77)*6: 108–118.

Herrington, G. T., Malone, P. T., & Georges, J. (2008). *Cracking the code to leadership.* Infinity.

Joyce, W., Nohria, N., & Robertson, B. (2003). *What really works.* Harper Business.

Juran, J. M. (2002). A Call to Action: The Summit. *Measuring Business Excellence (6)*3.

Kaplan, R. S., & Norton, D. P. (1996). *The balanced scorecard.* Harvard Business School Press.

Kehoe, L. (2002, March). Long live e-business: Software is finding a new role in helping companies to share information effectively. *Financial Times.*

Kotter, J. (1995). Leading change: Why transformation efforts fail. *Harvard Business Review (73)*2: 59–67.

Kotter, J. (1996). *Leading change.* Harvard Business School Press.

Kotter, J. (2001). What leaders really do. *Harvard Business Review (79)*11: 85–96.

Kotter, J. (2008). *A sense of urgency.* Harvard Business School Press.

Krames, J. A. (2008, October). Inside Drucker. *Leadership Excellence.*

Miles, R. H. (2010). Accelerating corporate transformations (don't lose your nerve). *Harvard Business Review (88)*1: 68–75.

Pfeffer, J., & Sutton, R. (2000). *The knowing-doing gap: How smart companies turn knowledge into action.* Harvard Business School Press.

Pfeffer, J., & Sutton, R. (2006). *Hard facts, dangerous half-truths and total non-sense: Profiting from evidence-based management.* Harvard Business School Press.

Porter, M. (1980). *Competitive strategy: Techniques for analyzing industries and competitors.* Free Press.

Porter, M. (1996). What is strategy? *Harvard Business Review (74)* 6: 61–78.

Ramias, A., & Wilkins, C. (2009, July). Varieties of process ownership. *BP Trends.*

Ross, J. W., & Weill, P. (2002). Six IT decisions your IT people shouldn't make. *Harvard Business Review (80)* 11: 84–92.

Rummler, G. A., & Brache, A. (1995). *Improving performance: How to manage the white space on the organization chart* (2nd ed.). Jossey-Bass.

Shapiro, B., Rangan, V. K., & Sviolka, J. J. (1992). Staple yourself to an order. *Harvard Business Review (70)*4: 113–122.

Smith, D., & Blakeslee, J., with Koonce, R. (2002). *Strategic Six Sigma: Best practices from the executive suite.* Wiley.

Spanyi, A. (2003). *Business process management is a team sport: Play it to win!* Anclote Press.

Spanyi, A. (2006). *More for less: The power of process management.* Meghan-Kiffer Press.

Stalk, G. (2008). *Five future strategies you need right now.* Harvard Business Press.

Swank, C. K. (2003, October). The Lean Service Machine, *Harvard Business Review (81)*10: 123–129.

Treacy, M., & Wiersema, F. (1995). *The discipline of market leaders.* Addison Wesley.

Index

www.ingramcontent.com/pod-product-compliance
Lightning Source LLC
Chambersburg PA
CBHW071515200326
41519CB00019B/5954